C000203187

Springer Wien New York

Sabine Seymour

Functional Aesthetics

Visions in Fashionable Technology

SpringerWien NewYork

Sabine Seymour
www.functionalaesthetics.org, www.moondial.com

This work is subject to copyright.
All rights are reserved, whether the whole or part of the material is concerned, specifically
those of translation, reprinting, re-use of illustrations, broadcasting, reproduction
by photocopying machines or similar means, and storage in data banks.

Product liability: The publisher can give no guarantee for the information contained
in this book. The use of registered names, trademarks, etc. in this publication does not
imply, even in the absence of a specific statement, that such names are exempt from the
relevant protective laws and regulations and are therefore free for general use.

This book is sponsored by

bm:uk

kunst universität linz
Universität für künstlerische und industrielle Gestaltung
www.ufg.ac.at

WIEN KULTUR

Bundesministerium für   Kunstuniversität Linz   Kulturabteilung der Stadt Wien,
Unterricht, Kunst und Kultur   Wissenschafts- und
                                                               Forschungsförderung

© 2010 Springer-Verlag/Wien. Printed in Austria
SpringerWienNewYork is a part of Springer Science+Business Media
springer.at

Graphic Design: Mahir Mustafa Yavuz
Research Assistance: Ricardo O'Nascimento
Copyediting & Proof Reading: Peter Blakeney & Christine Schöffler
Printing and binding: Holzhausen Druck GmbH, Vienna
Printed on acid-free and chlorine-free bleached paper

SPIN: 12764570
Library of Congress Control Number: 2010934299

With 160 illustrations
ISBN 978-3-7091-0311-1 SpringerWienNewYork

Contents

QR code tags are everywhere. On my last visit to Tokyo, it was apparent that QR codes are ubiquitous. They merge physical space with the virtual space of the Internet by instantly retrieving a website.

To find out more about the project, scan the QR code using an appropriate reader on your mobile phone.

Preface

Fashionable technology calls for visions that spring forth from progressive thinking and contextualized experiences. This book captures the inspiring breadth of topics engaged in the process of crafting fashionable technology as a creative practice, an industry, and a valid research area. The year 2010 appears to be the juncture when fashionable technology is elevated from the phase of experimentation. Currently, it is experiencing a boost from the fashion world's interest to be part of an exciting and exploratory field that bares many possibilities for creative investigation. Additionally, significant advances in technology and material science afford the creation of fashionable wearables that work in their proposed context of use and balance aesthetics and function.

The selected projects show the importance of interdisciplinary synergies, whether they are based in art or design, are commercial products, or seem to be explorations into wonder worlds. But at their core, they are professional, functional, aesthetically pleasing, and convey a story. The comprehensive encyclopedia of projects and lists of materials, publications, blogs and websites, institutions, and events in my previous book are extended with a supplementary bibliography, kits and DIY resources, and inspirations accumulated from the contributors.

This book is an attempt to solicit a collection of inspiring projects and resources, and stimulate a critical discourse.

Garment Graffiti by Thomas Voorn

Theoretical Discussion

Functional aesthetics

"Fashionable technology refers to the intersection of design, fashion, science, and technology."[1]

Functional aesthetics describes the concept of merging a fashionable technology object deemed aesthetically pleasant with technically enhanced functionalities.

"Fashionable wearables are 'designed' garments, accessories, or jewelry that combine aesthetics and style with functional technology."[2]

A synergy between the fields of fashion, design, science, and technology will create a future already envisioned in movies and science fiction stories, one that is rapidly becoming reality. The potential for collaboration between the worlds of fashion and technology has been omnipresent since the initial explorations of Hussein Chalayan ten years ago, notably the Remote Control Dress from 2000, and expanded into scientific experiments with the spray-on fabric Fabrican by trained fashion designer Manel Torres. The excursions into technology by another fashion designer, Gareth Pugh for a HSBC's advert from 2008, revealed the potential for further advances.

---

1   Seymour (2008a:12)

2   Seymour (2008a:12)

It is important to recognize the value of the word 'fashion', pointing out that aesthetics and style have been an obvious tool for the communication of values, culture, status, and mood individually over time. "Garments are the immediate interface to the environment and thus are constant transmitters and receivers of emotion, experiences, and meaning."[3] The issue of beauty, style, and aesthetics is important for the acceptance and commercial success of fashionable wearables. Regardless of the tremendous communication aspects of fashion, it has rarely enjoyed a very good reputation in the past. "Despite its undeniable success as a social and commercial phenomenon, it remains the very exemplum of superficiality, frivolity and vanity."[4]

The success of fashionable wearables relies on professional execution, from design to manufacturing to diffusion. Technically enhanced pants cannot be taken off on the street to be rebooted. Fashionable wearables have to work. The wearer simply does not expect it to fail. The technical integration needs to be seamless and invisible for the wearer. However, the inherently human desire to control and fear of abuse need to be revisited in this process, providing the ability for the user to consciously turn it off. Technology and scientific advances modify or enhance functions like heat regulation, impact protection, communication, antimicrobials, fire protection, etc. Technology is adding another layer of functionality to the garment, informed by craftsmanship and the exploration of novel materials. Thus, a closer collaboration with materials companies is necessary to enable the dissemination of know-how and to create stylish and functional fashionable wearables.

---

3   Seymour (2008a:12)

4   Vinken (2005:137)

Fashion'able' technology & fashionable wearables

The term fashion'able' technology refers to technology with an aesthetic appeal. The geek chic of the mid to late 90s and the appearance of wearable computing on a larger scale called for style, fashion, and aesthetics. The focus of the term is on 'able' with the intention of making technology fashionable and aesthetically pleasant. Particularly, the merging of virtual and physical spaces demands stylish avatars that live in both realities. Fashionable technology is associated with an array of disciplines in the fields of design and technology that frequently intersect. The significance of fashionable technology as an emerging field is apparent.

The use of the word 'technology' in fashionable technology needs clarification. Technologists coming from electrical engineering

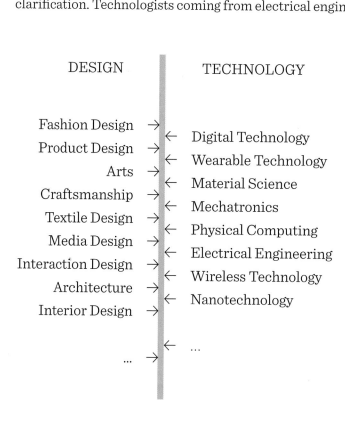

DESIGN   TECHNOLOGY

Fashion Design → ← Digital Technology
Product Design → ← Wearable Technology
Arts → ← Material Science
Craftsmanship → ← Mechatronics
Textile Design → ← Physical Computing
Media Design → ← Electrical Engineering
Interaction Design → ← Wireless Technology
Architecture → ← Nanotechnology
Interior Design →

... → ← ...

or multimedia often use the term with reference solely to digital technology, whereas a biotechnologist might see the definition of technology in a broader material-based sense. Fashionable technology refers to all technologies interlinked with the body like biotechnology, nanotechnology, digital technology, textile technology, etc. Additionally, it refers to tools and software applications associated with textile technologies and fashion design.

The necessity to engage the fashion world with the creation of fashionable wearables that capture the market and create a new set of high quality products is apparent. They can be a product (in private economy), an art piece or commission (in arts/cultural economy), or a prototype (in research). Fashionable wearables are the intermediary between the human body and the spaces we navigate. Our clothing, accessories, and jewelry are the epidermal interfaces with which we can experience the world. Data exchange is possible through the advances in wireless technologies, enabling communication among bodies and the space in which they reside, namely with reference to smart architecture. Fashionable wearables thus extend to architectural objects.

BODY

BODY/BODY/BODY

BODY—SPACE

BODY/BODY/BODY—SPACE

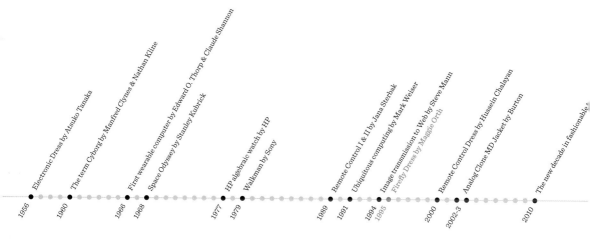

The timeline entries (left to right):

1956 — Electronic Dress by Atsuko Tanaka
1960 — The term Cyborg by Manfred Clynes & Nathan Kline
1966 — First wearable computer by Edward O. Thorp & Claude Shannon
1968 — Space Odyssey by Stanley Kubrick
1977 — HP algebraic watch by HP
1979 — Walkman by Sony
1989 — Remote Control I & II by Jana Sterbak
1991 — Ubiquitous computing by Mark Weiser
1994 — Image transmission to Web by Steve Mann
1995 — Firefly Dress by Maggie Orth
2000 — Remote Control Dress by Hussein Chalayan
2002-3 — Analog Clone MD Jacket by Burton
2010 — The new decade in fashionable *

An attempt at a timeline

The timeline of fashionable technology is strongly intertwined with
the history of wearable computing. The potential for collaboration
between the worlds of fashion and technology has been ever-present
since the initial explorations by Hussein Chalayan ten years ago with
the Remote Control Dress in 2000. It marked the extension of 'soft
computation' into garments – a field that previously seemed solely a
computing and engineering domain not engaged in issues of the body
or wearability. Soft computation is described by Joanna Berzowska
as the "design of digital and electronic technology that is composed
of soft materials such as textiles and yarns, as well as predicated
on traditional construction methods to create interactive physical
designs."[5]

Electronically enhanced garments as artistic expression were
developed much earlier. In 1956, the Japanese artist Atsuko Tanaka
created the Electronic Dress. The first mention of a human being
augmented with technological attachments was by Manfred Clynes
and co-author Nathan Kline who coined the term 'cyborg' in 1960.
In 1966, Edward O. Thorp and Claude Shannon developed the first

---

5   Berzowska (2005:67)

known battery-run, mobile and wearable computer for predicting gambling results.[6] In this period, visionary depictions of fashion were provided by films such as Stanley Kubrick's 2001: A Space Odyssey from 1968.

A decade later, in 1977, Hewlett-Packard released the HP algebraic watch. It was followed by Sony's introduction of the Walkman in 1979: the first portable music player, a phenomenon that extends up to the MP3 format today. In 1980, Steve Mann, the creator of wearable computing, built a head-mounted CRT (cathode ray tube) prototype. The sculptural artistic works by Jana Sterbak often took the form of garment-like constructions. The projects Remote Control I & II from 1989 consisted of a motorized metal crinoline operated with a remote control.

In 1994, Steve Mann began transmitting images from a head-mounted camera to the Web. This was made possible by the overwhelming developments in ubiquitous computing, which Mark Weiser described in 1991 as a world in which most everyday objects have computational devices embedded in them.[7] The Firefly Dress & Necklace by Maggie Orth with Emily Copper and Derek Lockwood in 1995 marks the beginning of fashionable technology. "As the wearer moves, the Velcro contacts the conductive fabric and causes the LEDs to light."[8] However, this project was still developed by an artist and engineer rather than conceived by a fashion designer.

For the 2002–2003 winter season, Burton released the Analog Clone MD Jacket with an integrated Sony MP3 player. The fabric of the jacket had electronic switching capabilities made possible by combining conductive textile materials and flexible composites.

---

6   Seymour, Beloff (2008)

7   Seymour (2008a)

8   Seymour (2008a:76)

It marked the introduction of fashionable technology in noticeable consumer products.

2010 proclaims the beginning of a new decade in fashionable technology with the launch of numerous commercially successful products, highly visible commissioned projects and installations, and advances in technologies and materials.

Fashionable wearables as viable artifacts

Experimental projects represent a test bed for fashionable wearables. Hussein Chalayan tapped into technology as a means of expression as a fashion designer. The inspiring pieces are conceptual and have a performance character. They demonstrate the need for innovative design and fantasy in the creation of fashionable wearables to excite the wearer. The main focus of researchers, designers, and artists has long been on advances in technologies rather than creating appealing propositions for consumers. Today, technologies have matured and range from mechatronics to nanotechnology. These innovations will shape the future of clothing. Much of the essential technology is already available to create meaningful and commercially viable products.

Clothing with embedded technologies is evident in the realms of sport, work wear, healthcare and rehabilitation, rescue services, elderly care, and security. Consumer interest in fashionable wearables is steadily increasing. Their success is determined by a product's ability to capture human emotion by meeting a need and its aesthetic performance. Personalization of fashionable wearables allows for new modes of self-expression, which is an essential factor in making fashion items that appeal to the public. The expertise needed to successfully bring products to the market is a unique skill set that combines market know-how, product development, user aspirations, available technology, manufacturing resources, legal ramifications, and cost structures. Designers must have a comprehensive understanding of the purpose, the user, the interaction, and – for commercial applications – the right price point. An appealing design in combination with an intuitive interface and suitable materials will make for a successful fashionable wearable.

The design of an intelligent garment is complex because of the breadth of disciplines needed in its development. Most projects that are currently being developed on a larger scale use various subcontractors. A consolidation would reduce costs, simplify the communication and project management process, and have only one or a few suppliers to monitor quality and deal with warranty issues. Thus, specialized design and production studios need to be established. Additionally, a common vocabulary is evolving to allow efficient and fruitful collaboration between disciplines, such as physical computing, fashion design, industrial design, wireless networking, software engineering, and graphic design.

The three main modules for creating marketable fashionable wearables are strongly intertwined.

› Collection
Information about materials, technologies and technical feasibility, trends, user aspirations, context of use, precedents and competition, recyclability, energy supply, wearability, manufacturing resources, sustainability, legal ramifications, etc. is assembled.

› Configuration

The assembled knowledge is then configured for the creation of the defined products. This includes the actual design and preparations for the production, the creation of mood boards and fashion illustrations, through to the technical design adaptation by defining and producing the software and hardware modules.

› Integration

The configured technology and materials are integrated. This production process ranges from the prototype to the final product. Concurrent engineering takes place after usability analysis, the testing of the technical functionality, and the evaluation of the wearability until a golden sample for the final manufacturing is derived.

The diffusion of a fashionable wearable is dependent on the perceived usefulness and technical ease of use. Thus, users need to experience its functionalities and receive informed explanations.

Novel forms of display for fashionable wearables

Fashionable wearables need to be exhibited differently to reveal all of their features and stimulate the audience's senses in immersive experiences. The following description acts as a proposal:

> *London's Dover Street Market &*
> *Paris' L'Eclaireur meet*
> *Apple's Genius Bar*

Dover Street Market is a multistory fashion store conceived by Rei Kawakubo in London's posh Dover Street setting. The visual appearance of each floor is different with a distinct interior design fitting for the garments on sale. Posh, trendy, punk, rather slick, you name it. The music changes from rock in the basement to a more pop sound on the upper floor. There is a subtle smell of perfume on the first floor whereas the top story has the scent of fresh baked goods. It is a multisensory experience.

Set in trendy Marais in Paris, L'Eclaireur is not a modest shop rather a remarkable interactive installation created by Arne Quinze with 147 animated video screens. The Room Book by Electronic Shadow is a separate space within the shop with digital projects that are like chapters of an evolving book. Through personal attention every visitor undergoes a specific experience. It is a great balance of shop and gallery.

The Apple Genius Bar in Apple Stores offers comfort, advice, and expertise and reduces the aggravation users of technical devices often experience.

The new form of display for fashionable wearables requires a multisensory, tangible user experience with personalization and explanation by educated personnel. A retailer of fashionable wearables needs to provide an immersive experience with no real delineation between a store and a gallery.

CHAPTER 01

Body Sculpture

Body modifications and augmentations are a cultural phenomenon. In medicine, the line between necessary modifications and implants is blurred by cultural and social implications. Pace makers, screws and plates, and implanted hearing devices are well received, and ethical issues are little discussed due to the direct impact on one's well-being. The debate starts over beauty surgery and body augmentations. The physique of the body might inspire the shape of a garment or an accessory. The advent of aging and advances in rehabilitation spur the need for prosthesis support in the form of designed objects that fulfill a very specific physical function but are aesthetically appealing and have a modest psychological impact for the wearer.

Stelarc's Ear in Arm, Engineering Internet Organ project from 2008 blurs the boundaries with the mediated implant. For the project, Stelarc surgically implanted an ear, which will be further equipped with a microphone to allow the wireless transmission of sounds captured by the ear to a distant location. According to Stelarc, "the final procedure will re-implant a miniature microphone to enable a wireless connection to the Internet, making the ear a remote listening device for people in other places"[1].

The subsequent projects provide aesthetic inspirations, using the body as a basis for the created sculptures. Most of the projects do not employ any digital technology but provide visions for the design of a human robot through examining and styling the human physique.

---

1   www.stelarc.va.com.au/projects/earonarm/index.html

Hussein Chalayan
Inertia 2009 /
Earthbound 2009

The implications of architecture on the body are illustrated with concrete structures, enabling a new conceptualization of 'soft'.

Hussein graduated in 1993 from London's Central St. Martins School of Art and Design and launched his own label in 1994. He uses film, installations, and sculptural forms to explore perception and realities of modern life, with particular interest in cultural identity, migration, anthropology, technology, nature, and genetics. His work is presented at his shows and in art galleries, while his clothing is available in boutiques worldwide. Sponsored by Turquality, he represented Turkey in the 2005 Venice Biennale with Absent Presence featuring Tilda Swinton. The Groninger Museum in the Netherlands and the London Design Museum hosted a massive retrospective of his work in 2005 and 2009 respectively.

Inertia

Keywords: fashion, architecture, sculpture, speed

"Finally the body became the 'event' of a crash where garments caught in the midst of speed simultaneously embodied the cause and effect of a crash in one moment." (Hussein Chalayan) The final pieces of Inertia 2009 are sculpture dresses made from molded foam and wrapped with flexible heat transfer prints of car bodywork and molded to look as though they are crystallized in motion.

Architecture, structures, and building processes and materials all play an integral role in the translation from concept into clothing. In the Earthbound collection, bright turquoise and coral embellished prints of scaffolding and stone move into a section of specially created, vibrantly

Earthbound

colored molded leather busts and bottoms
attached to soft concrete print leather
dresses. These elements are incorporated
to create the impression of architecture,
blurring the gap between reality and fantasy.

www.husseinchalayan.com

Amy Thompson
Plastic Analogue

Plastic Analogue strikes to convey a new aesthetic for body-encasing garments and blurs the line between robotics and fashion.

Amy Thompson is a concept-led fashion designer (MA Fashion Bodywear graduate of De Montfort University) who seeks to explore the unknown, achieve the unexpected, challenge the existing, and create the extraordinary. Innovation in her work is achieved in the fusion of contemporary and traditional techniques, the crossover into non-fashion disciplines, and the use of unconventional materials. Amy allows creative experimentation to direct and shape each piece she designs, often using sculptural methods to exaggerate and manipulate silhouette and scale.

Keywords: translucent, body-encasing,
flat-pack, robotics, armor

Plastic Analogue was produced at De Montfort University, Leicester, UK in September 2008. It is a striking array of sculpted silhouettes that encase the body with protective interlocking armor that fuses innovative technology, product design, and fashion to a dynamic effect. Flat-pack construction techniques create an alternative and unique method of manipulating exaggerated armor-inspired polypropylene structures into contemporary interlocking garments and accessories, while sections of specially designed lenticular lens technology are used to provide visually hypnotic and oscillating patterns that spin and change color according to which angle the garment is viewed from. The plastic armor is created using polypropylene and lenticular technology; for the digitally printed fabric garments Lycra and silk habotai are used.

www.amyjthompson.com

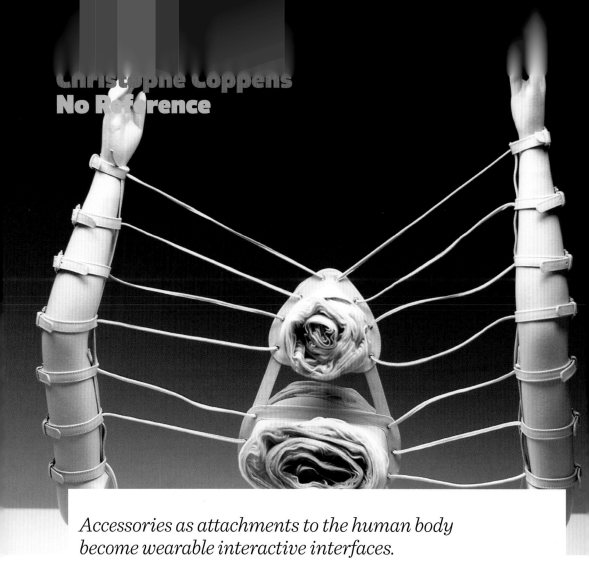

Accessories as attachments to the human body become wearable interactive interfaces.

Christophe Coppens was born in Belgium in 1969 and trained as a theater director and actor. He was soon directing his own plays as well as designing the costumes. In 1990, he opened his own studio and began producing two collections a year. He made hats for Yohji Yamamoto and Guy Laroche, began working with the Belgian royal family, made exhibitions and performances in Belgium, the Netherlands, Tokyo, and New York, started

an interior products range, and opened shops in Belgium and Japan. His second couture collection was exhibited in the Steenfabriek at the 2007 Arnhem Fashion Biennale.

Keywords: sculpture, exhibition, body, accessories

Christophe Coppens received the first H+F Fashion Award to realize No Reference, a

project comprising an accessories collection, a book, and an exhibition held at Platform 21 in Amsterdam from 2008-09. Coppens took the award as an opportunity to question his own work. He has gone back to square one, abandoning all baggage: No Reference. Or, as philosopher Pieter van Bogaert writes in the introduction to the book No Reference: "You throw everything overboard – all references within your own work, all references to books and artists, all references within fashion, to material and its connotations, to techniques, to form. You aim to take a new look at the accessory's raison d'être, its purpose. You want to use this opportunity to go back to the essence of the design, to think, and to explore. It's not about 'What can I do differently, better, more beautifully, more extravagantly?' Or 'What can I add or take away?' It's about: 'What is a color? What is a shape? What is an accessory? What is a fashion? What is a body? [...] You throw all your references overboard and then see what happens. Allow the things to live. Let your clients finish the work. Everyone, producer and user, is equal. The imagination rules."

www.christophecoppens.com
www.hfcollection.org
www.platform21.nl

Francesca Lanzavecchia
ProAesthetics Supports

Body extensions, how they are perceived, and the opportunities of using technology to enhance the use of such aids are facets of the future human-centered design practice.

Francesca Lanzavecchia, born in Pavia, Italy in 1983, earned a degree in product design from the Politecnico di Milano in 2005. In 2006, she worked in the Department of Trends & Views of Decathlon. In 2008, she obtained a Masters of Design Cum Laude from the Design Academy Eindhoven, The Netherlands. Her work has been presented in internationally renowned periodicals and publications. Recently, she was awarded the Time to Design - New Talent Award by the Danish Ministry of Culture.

Keywords: disability, aesthetics, imperfection, desirability, identity

With her thesis work ProAesthetics Supports: The Perception of Disability through its Artifacts, – produced in Eindhoven in 2008 – Lanzavecchia manages to rehumanize disability aids and transform them into desirable objects instead of objects of shame. We live in a world where there are thousands of styles of jeans to choose from, but only a few models of wheelchairs. In our society, people with disabilities are not offered the chance to choose and express themselves. They are offered aids with mechanical and generic body accessories that emphasize only the technical aspect. In this way, the aid objects become a sign of social stigma and in no way help the subject to recover a new and acceptable identity. The ProAesthetics Supports project looks into the perception of disability through its artifacts. It does so by researching user-object relationships and behaviors, self-image versus public-image, and the aesthetic-functional language of disability aids. This research brought Francesca Lanzavecchia to create a series of medical aids that retain full functionality but adapt different styles to match the wish of the user. Lanzavecchia's project is an invitation to lightness and to playfulness; these orthoses, braces, and canes become tools to speak about the illness or about the ill body in ways that are relevant to their users.

www.francesca.nu

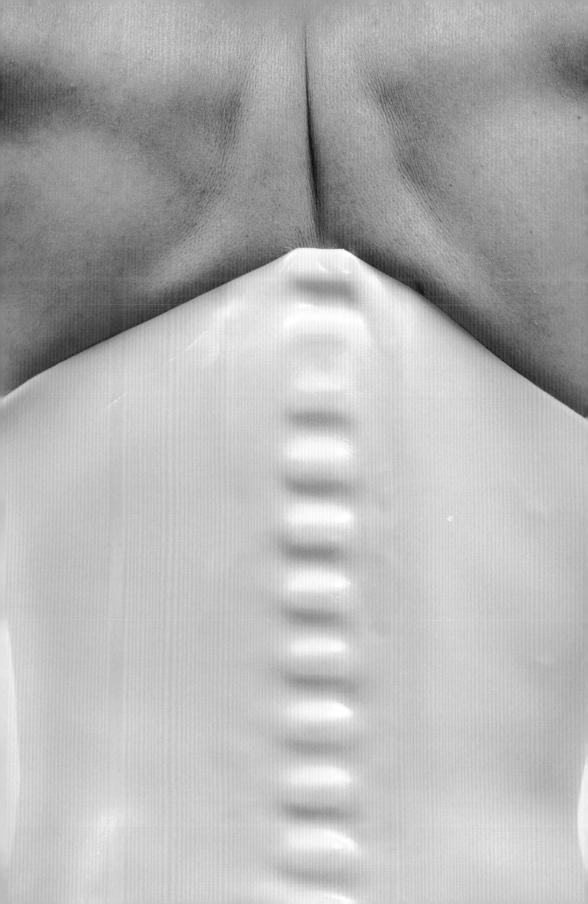

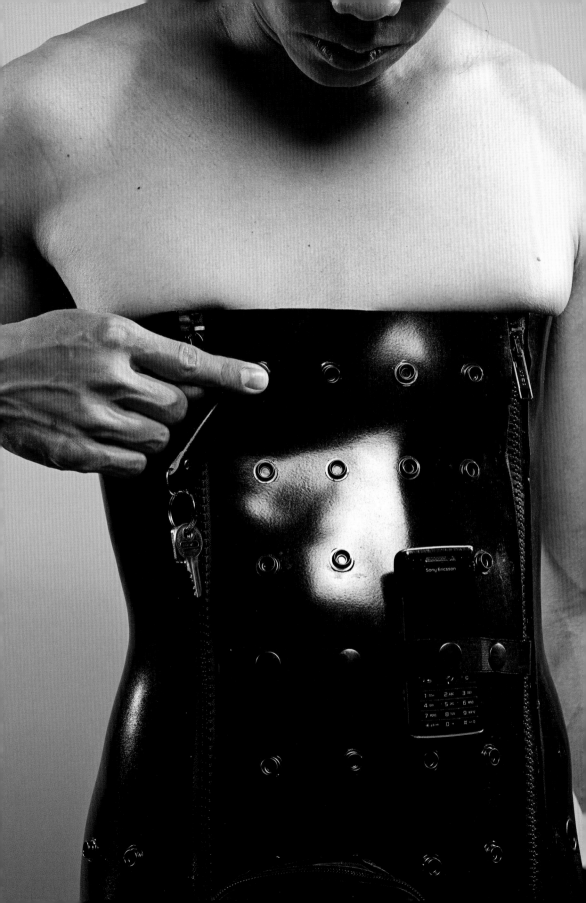

Úna Burke
Re.treat

Re.treat demonstrates the importance of applied craftsmanship and its implications for wearability and body sculpture.

Úna Burke is an artist and designer specialized in traditional leatherworking techniques. She was born, raised, and studied fashion to BA level in Ireland. After working with several Irish designers, Úna moved to London in 2006. She worked with Philip Treacy, Burberry, and Smythson, among others, and then completed an MA in fashion artefact at London College of Fashion. Her final collection, a series of wearable, sculptural leather forms, has appeared in Vogue Italia, Numero, Dazed and Confused, and Harpers Bazaar, and icons such as Lady Gaga, Daphne Guinness, and Madonna have also requested her work.

Keywords: emotional, intricate, provocative, sculpture, medical braces, body

This conceptual collection depicts eight human gestures associated with the cause, the psychological aftermath, and the healing

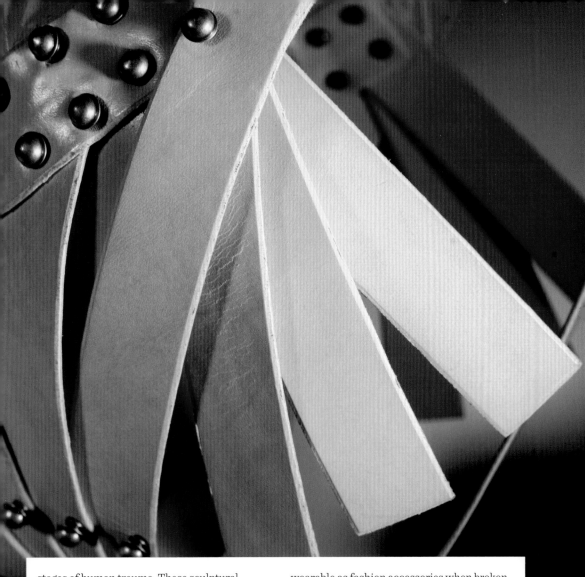

stages of human trauma. These sculptural forms are created around the shape of a contorted female body. A number of pieces are reminiscent of medical braces, signifying the potential for healing within the boundaries of something that inhibits the body. Each carcass-like piece is handcrafted from vegetable tanned leather, resulting in a color indicative of human flesh. Produced as contemplation artifacts to be viewed in a gallery environment, these objects are also wearable as fashion accessories when broken down into sections, such as arm, leg, head, neck, and shoulder pieces. The collection was produced in London, UK in 2008. Materials used include undyed vegetable tanned cow hide leather, sponsored by Grade Leather, and tarnished brass fittings and screws.

www.unaburke.com

GAIA
VEASYBLE – Unfold a beautiful intimacy

The psychological intent of transformation is accomplished through a simple yet striking design.

GAIA design is an atelier, an experimental lab for the 'staging' of design in a limited series, born in 2008 during the final year of a degree course at ISIA Florence in Italy. GAIA is Gloria Pizzilli, Arianna Petrakis, Ilaria Pacini, and Adele Bacci, a heterogeneous group of four designers, temperamentally very different but unexpectedly cohesive and harmonic in terms of design. Three product designers and one communication designer attain a 360° conception of design.

Keywords: isolation, intimacy, ornament, paper

VEASYBLE is a 4-piece collection of wearable design accessories for unfolding your contextual presence into a state of beautiful intimacy. VEASYBLE is made of paper bonded to polyethylene and fabric.

A common folded pattern shapes each VEASYBLE piece, which can vary in scale and proportion according to the desired intimacy. A ruff that becomes a hood. A headband that becomes a mask. A barrette that becomes a visor. A bag that becomes a shell. The idea is inspired by the changes in our bodily relationships with the public environment: Departing from the effects of our increased intersubjectivity and interpersonal life, GAIA explores how our sense of intimacy creates new demands.

www.veasyble.com

Philips
Fractal: Living Jewelry

Digital technology extends and enhances the human body's ability to sense, thereby offering limitless applications.

Philips Design Probes is a dedicated 'far-future' research initiative at Philips in Eindhoven, The Netherlands, which tracks trends and developments that may ultimately evolve into mainstream issues and have a significant impact on business. With the aim of understanding 'lifestyle' post-2020, the program aims to identify probable systemic shifts in social and economic domains likely to affect business and create intellectual property in new areas. It challenges conventional ways of thinking to come up with concepts that stimulate debate. Deliverables range from scenarios and narratives to the creation of experience prototypes and IP fortressing.

Keywords: emotional sensing, jewelry, light, hybrid

As part of the ongoing Design Probes Program, Fractal, produced in August 2008,

continues the theme of the body as a platform for electronic functionalities and explores 'analog' phenomena, such as emotional sensing and sensitive technology. Fractal is 'living jewelry' as it has a range of behaviors that are stimulated by muscle tension and proximity. Performance sensing technologies enable integrated LED light to detect changes in the wearer's muscle tension and movement as well as other people in close proximity and to respond by pulsing. In terms of design, Philips Design was interested in the fusion of apparel and jewelry; technically, the challenge was to achieve specific effects using hybrid materials and biometric sensing. The aim was to create an apparel body piece manufactured with non-textile materials and non-apparel assembly methods.

www.design.philips.com/philips/sites/philipsdesign/probes/projects/fractal/index.page

Naomi Filmer
Chocolate Mask / Shoulder Ball Lense

Chocolate Mask

Explorations with materials enable inspiring solutions for technology-enhanced body ornamentation and jewelry.

Based in Milan, Italy, Naomi Filmer is a contemporary jewelry designer who describes her work as 'wearable objects about the body' rather than jewelry. After studying 3D design, she completed a master's degree in goldsmithing, silversmithing, metalwork, and jewelry at the Royal College of Art, London. She acquired a reputation in the 1990s for catwalk collaborations with high-profile British designers such as Hussein Chalayan, Shelley Fox, and Alexander McQueen. Her experimental use of materials (ice, chocolate, glass, and rubber) underlines a focus on the qualities and value of the body and of flesh. By combining craftsmanship with new media and exploring recurrent themes such as fragmentation and isolation of the body, Filmer attempts to push the boundaries of art and accessories, creating objects that occupy a middle ground between art and design.

Keywords: body, jewelry, materials, exploration, craftsmanship

Chocolate Mask was produced in London in 2001 with the Elisabeth Shaw Chocolate company by casting chocolate into a silicone mold before attaching the gold-plated silver mouthpiece. Working with chocolate was part of a series of her works, where the experience of wearing objects is seen as precious, rather than object material alone. Chocolate melts at body temperature, demonstrating the wearer as the dominant value factor. The object life is limited, and yet the experience of wearing it reaches our senses of taste and touch, of consumption and sensuality. The Mask was made for a shoot in the 2nd issue of Another Magazine, photographed by Richard Burbridge.

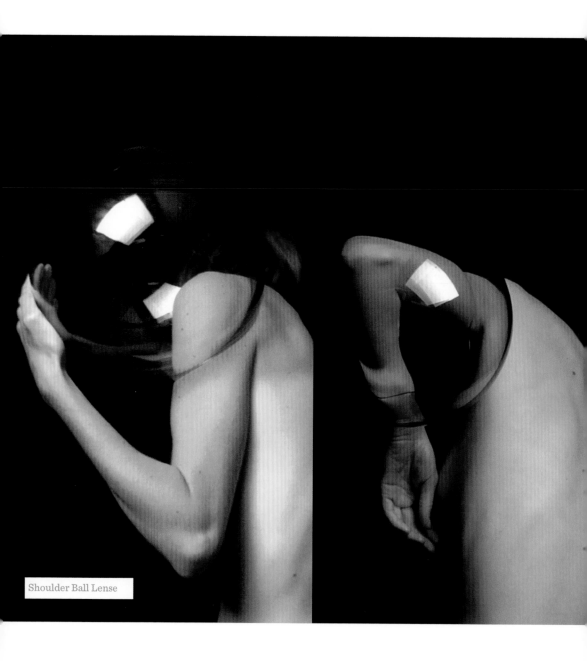

Shoulder Ball Lense

Keywords: emotional sensing, jewelry, light, hybrid

Shoulder Ball Lense was exhibited at Out of the Ordinary, The Spectacular Craft at the V&A Museum in London in 2007. As a response to the theme, Naomi created an installation presenting 10 parts of the human anatomy as jewels in their own right. Each body part is set into glass spheres, which effectively function as a lens to focus on extraordinary details of ourselves. The images are frames from film loops made to create a series of lenticulars that demonstrate a focus and distortion of body parts inside the glass spheres.

www.naomifilmer.co.uk

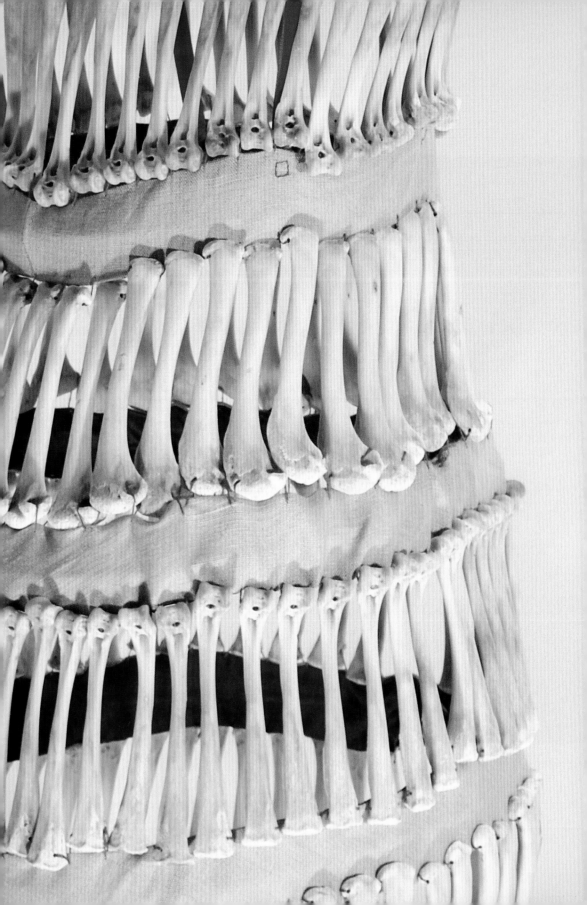

Käthe Wenzel
Bone Dress

Advances in the creation of artificial body sculptures investigate the ergonomics of the human body shaped through the process of evolution.

Wenzel explores the collective production of culture, the interface of art and science, and the production and negotiation of public space. She studied in Marburg, Florence, and Berlin and received a PhD in 2005 for the dissertation Meat as Materials in Art. She is a Fulbright visiting professor at SVA in New York, lecturer in Vienna and Bremen, and lives in Berlin. Her garment-objects deal with the topographical survey of bodies and attempt to define the body's perimeter in a time when traditional concepts of 'body', 'nature', or 'technology' are becoming obsolete and when divisions between 'body' and 'garment' are becoming blurred.

Keywords: exoskeleton, body extension, customized body, physical discipline

The Bone Dress from 2005 revisits the term 'fully boned', which describes a completely stiffened corset. Taken literally, 'fully boned' results in a wearable exoskeleton that reverses the habitual sequence of layers – dress, flesh, bone – and suggests an even more basic inversion of concepts. The corset itself is a tool for shaping and disciplining unruly (female) bodies. Today, new technologies are being developed to tailor bodies according to beauty standards. The bone garment can also be seen as a physical add-on, an organic extension for future bodies that can be extended or reduced thanks to technologies that completely dissolve traditional distinctions between 'body' and 'artifact', 'nature', 'fashion', or 'technology'. The Bone Dress is made of silk, canvas, duck bones, synthetic thread, and a wicker.

www.kaethewenzel.de/html/
englkostueme.htm

CHAPTER 02

The Garment as Amplifier of Fantasy

The expressive value of fashionable wearables can be greatly heightened through the integration of technology. By incorporating electronics into a garment, we can transform traditional fashion elements such as color, texture, and cut to include movement, touch, light, sound, and interactivity as new aesthetic interaction interfaces. This novel characteristic of being dynamic spurs imaginations that far exceed current explorations.

The Sound Suit by the Austrian artist Bernhard Leitner[1] from 1975 uses the different reactions of bones, muscles, skin, arteries, and soft tissue as acoustic impulses to create a sound-space sculpture. The suit is covered by a fine-meshed net that forms a neutral grid, enabling the attachment of loudspeakers at any point of the body. The Sound Suit literally amplifies one's fantasy – similar to that of Inspector Gadget, the main character in the TV comic series produced from 1983 to 1986. Inspector Gadget's garments and accessories became immediate interactive tools that possess different functions. I was most inspired by the fact that he could fly; an ability already chronicled in the 1920s with the appearance of Buck Rogers in the science fiction magazine Amazing Stories.

---

1   www.bernhardleitner.com/de/plus/tona75/ton75_1.html

The following visionary examples include garments that interface with the environment through digital technology, the augmentation of physical reality, or purely through mechanics or environmental data. They are garments that amplify the human imagination, pieces that identify the psychological functions of fashionable wearables.

Hussein Chalayan
Grains and Steel A/W 2008

Showpieces by proficient fashion designers facilitate exciting explorations of technology.

→ Biography on page 22

Keywords: light, body, human evolution

Grains and Steel is yet another collaboration between Hussein Chalayan and Swarovski. As Chalayan describes: "The collection represents an abstract story book depicting evolution. The body, conveyed through print and texture, acts as a tool first portraying non-existence, then the Big Bang and various stages involving water, life, the apes, agricultural societies, and those conquests enabled by steel and guns." The collection description notes that the subject of human evolution is the key influence this season, seen from a biological, political, social, and technological perspective.

www.husseinchalayan.com

Ricardo O'Nascimento & Tiago Martins
Rambler Shoes

Rambler Shoes invokes the promise of new interactive interfaces and the augmentation of reality through social networking.

Ricardo O'Nascimento is an artist, multimedia developer, and producer who works at the intersection between fashion and technology. He is a graduate in international relations from PUC-SP and multimedia design from Art Center SENAC–SP, Brazil, and has a master's in Interface Culture from the University of Arts Linz, Austria. He investigates body-environment relations with a focus on interface development and autonomous adaptive systems for interactive installations, worn devices, and hybrid environments.

Tiago Martins graduated in computer science at the Universidade Nova de Lisboa (FCT-UNL) and worked as a research assistant in geo-referenced media and interactive narratives at the Research Center for Informatics and Information Technologies (CITI). He is currently a PhD candidate at Interface Culture at the University of Arts Linz where he is also a guest teacher. He co-authors interactive installations and media art projects, which playfully explore bonds between the physical, digital, and social.

Keywords: wearable electronics, Web 2.0, Twitter, social network

Rambler is a critical take on near-obsessive microblogging habits, stimulating reflection on the personal nature, amount, and usefulness of the information generated everyday by blogging and social platforms such as Twitter. This project presents a pair of sneakers that take microblogging one step further by literally posting your steps on a Twitter account. Messages are composed of the word "tap" and ".", which represent the wearer's steps and the period of time in between respectively. Rambler Shoes was created in Linz in 2010.

www.popkalab.com/ramblershoes.html

UdK Berlin, Daniel Schulze & Hannah Wiesener
e-Motion: White Pages

Collaborative projects in a university context enable technical experimentation and advanced fashion design.

e-MOTION was a one-year project carried out at the Fashion and Textile Design Institute at Berlin University of the Arts in Germany (UdK) during the 2008/09 academic year. The project name stands for the interaction of emotion, motion, and electronics with reference to the human body. Ten students from fashion, product and interface design departments within the Design Faculty at UdK were involved in this project. Two of the projects are featured.

The teaching staff consisted of Prof. Valeska Schmidt-Thomsen, Institute of Fashion and Textile Design, UdK; Prof. Holger Neumann, Institute of Product Design, UdK; Christina Kleßmann, Institute of Fashion and Textile Design, UdK; Jana Patz, Institute of Fashion and Textile Design, UdK; Prof. Dr. Zane Berzina, research fellow, Digital Studios and Constance Howard Resource and Research Centre in Textiles, Goldsmiths, University of London, UK. Project partners were Fraunhofer Institute for Reliability and Microintegration, IZM/Berlin, Germany; Dipl. Ing. Christian Dils, Institute for Special Textiles and Flexible Materials – TITV Greiz,

Germany; Dr. Andreas Neudeck, specialist printing pigments, Cornelius Industrial Group, UK. Guests were Javier Ferreira Gonzalez, Madrid/Boras, Lucy McRae, Eindhoven, and Di Mainstone, London.

Keywords: fashion, interactivity, emotion, art, media

Texture and textile – every garment carries a certain story for its wearer. Like a second skin, the narrative layer lies under the garment's surface and escorts us during the day. Through a special combination of different materials and an adhesive effect of targeted pressure, the first coat can transform into an analogue message board. The second coat comprises a complete media cycle: recording, converting, and projecting images. The wearer can take a picture of a situation during the day, which then is saved as a b/w 8x8 pixel image and translated into a flexible pleat matrix via shape memory technology. This picture is reserved for a private moment: It disappears with higher sound levels and becomes readable in silence. The soft pleat matrix serves as a display for a wide range of information.

UdK Berlin, Max Schäth
e-Motion: Outsourcing

Keywords: fashion, interactivity,
emotion, art, sensors, SMA

The aim was to create a garment that references
a person's senses and feelings in an abstract way.
Human feelings emerge from an accumulation of
sensations received by the conglomerate of senses.
The garment finds its emotional expression in the
transformation of the hood via integrated sensors
and shape memory alloys. No specific emotion is
represented, rather the repositioning of the hood
generates an awareness within the wearer, who can
then evaluate his or her own feelings in a novel way.

www.design.udk-berlin.de/Modedesign/Emotion

Di Mainstone
Serendiptichord

Performance is a great medium to explore reactions and spur fantasy in an encapsulated and innocent environment.

Di Mainstone designs wearable sculptures for exploratory performance. Visually ambiguous, these tactile adornments only reveal their full potential through the playful curiosity of the handler. In her work, Di enjoys collaborations with architects, musicians, mathematicians, and scientists across Europe and North America. Her unique choreography of fashion, technology, and performance draws clients from the worlds of art, fashion, dance, film, and music. Currently expanding her home practice in London, Di continues to exhibit, create, and lecture internationally.

Keywords: performance, instrument, wearable, choreophonic, sound

Serendiptichord was created in collaboration with The Centre for Digital Music, Queen Mary, University of London, under the Platform Grant (EPSRC grant EP/E045235/1) for the ACM Creativity and Cognition Conference 2009 and supported by the Interactional Sound and Music Group. Special thanks to Nick Bryan-Kinns and Mark Plumbley for their support and advice, to Niamh O'Connor, Judy Zhang, and Stacey Grant for creative assistance, and to Vesselin Iordanov for technical assistance. Sound design: Tim Murray-Brown; Creative assistant: Rachel Lamb

A result of cross-disciplinary investigation spanning fashion, technology, music, and dance, the Serendiptichord is a wearable musical instrument that entices the user to explore a soundscape through physical manipulation and expressive movement. Housed in a bespoke box, this alluring device is viewed as part of a performance when it is unpacked and explored on and around the body. Adhering to the body like an extended limb, this device is best described as 'choreophonic prosthetic'. It references the architectural silhouette of a musical instrument and the soft fabrication of fashion and upholstery. Although this acoustic device can be mastered alone, it also holds subtle incentives for group interaction.

www.dimainstone.com

Bart Hess
Hunt for High-Tech

Bart Hess is based in Einhoven, The Netherlands, and explores several fields that straddle material, animation, and photography within both the commercial and art worlds. Bart works in primitive and infinite ways: Instinctively, he starts with a material on the body, exploring volumes and ways of reshaping the human silhouette, at a fast speed, expelling all his creative energy. He develops imagery that captures future human shapes and new body forms. Bart is discovering a low-tech prosthetic method of human enhancement.

Keywords: animal, fur, low-tech

With a Hunt for High-Tech in 2007, Bart Hess made a collection of fake furs that touches on elements of fetishism, human instinct, and new animal archetypes. He did not mimic real animal kingdoms rather he created a

The merging of organic forms with robotics triggers fantasies long explored yet still appealing to the human imagination.

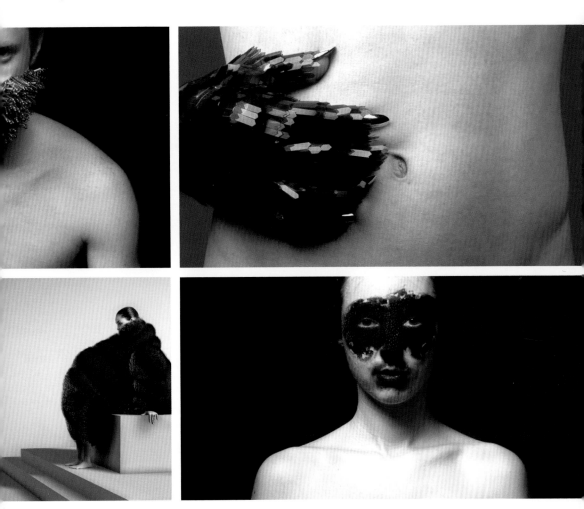

fantasy world of his own. The process began by imagining fantasy animals; animals that could be genetically manipulated, part robot, part organic, how they would move in their environment, and what they felt like to touch.

"I used materials that were not organic or commonly seen in the fashion world, together with blended plastics, metallics, silicones, and technical foils. I tried to manipulate

and recreate the same qualities and tactile feeling my fantasy animal kingdom has."

www.barthess.nl

Jennifer Darmour, Electricfoxy
Ping: A Social Networking Garment

*The garment becomes our immediate interface
with our environment using digital data.*

Jennifer Darmour is a Seattle-based wearable
technology designer who merges the
intimacy of clothing with the empowerment
of technology. Her company Electricfoxy
has developed a collection of projects
that investigate three important areas in
wearable technology: the connection to
larger software systems, aesthetics, and
marketability of wearable solutions. She
holds an MFA from Art Center College of
Design, Pasadena, CA. The team consisted
of Jesse Graupmann, developer; Tanya
Min Jee Ellis, apparel design; Peter Gaan,
photographer; and Karelea Mazzola, model.

*Keywords: wearable technology,
e-textiles, social network, aesthetics*

Ping: A Social Networking Garment is a
garment that connects to your Facebook
account wirelessly and from anywhere.

Created in 2010, it allows you to stay
connected to your friends and groups of
friends by simply performing natural gestures
that activate mechanisms built into the
garment: lift up a hood, tie a bow, zip, button,
simply move, bend and swing to ping your
friends naturally and automatically. No
phone, no laptop, no hardware. Simply go
about your day, look good, and stay connected.
Ping is composed of natural jersey knit,
Arduino Lilypad, Lilypad Xbee, flexible
sensors, vibration sensor, conductive thread,
custom software, and Facebook software.

www.electricfoxy.com/ping/

Martin Rille
Coded Sensation

Martin Rille studied at the Faculdade de Belas-Artes in Lisbon, Portugal, and wrote his diploma in transmedia art under Prof. Brigitte Kowanz at the University of Applied Arts Vienna, Austria. His studies on contact improvisation techniques across Europe informed the project Coded Sensation. He has worked on international research projects and realized several installations (Museum of Applied Arts Vienna, Technisches Museum Vienna) and video works (Museum of Modern Art Vienna, Museum of Contemporary Art Belgrade). In 2009, Coded Sensation was first demonstrated in an installation at the international Vienna Artfair. He collaborated with Max Frey, Amber Gabrielle, Sarah Hyee, and Hans Köcher.

Keywords: contact, digital skin, chrome dioxide, augmented sense

The skin as a protective organ, diaphragm, and container for physique and psyche: These metaphors manifest in Coded Sensation, an electromagnetic shell that carries coded information from magnetic tape cassettes.

The human skin has a large number of sensory capacities calling for a diverse set of sensors and actuators for the body.

An ultra-thin sheet of chrome dioxide can be applied to any kind of fabric surface, which stores information through magnetic modulation. Information – such as music, stories, and poems – can be written and read by touching the surface of these coded fabrics with a glove device, which is worn by the user as an adaptive sense. A reading head, consisting of an electromagnetic sense coil, reads the magnetic fluctuation in the chrome dioxide material. It then is transformed into an acoustic medium. Coded Sensation comprises clothes and interior seats covered with recorded audio tapes, gloves with audio pick-up, wireless microphones, computer, pure data, amplifiers, and speakers.

www.codedsensation.com
http://transmedialekunst.com/

Soomi Park
LED Eyelashes

Technology is used to exemplify a social phenomenon when fantasy becomes fetish.

Soomi Park is a multimedia artist and graphic designer based in Seoul, Korea. Her design work is driven by her curiosity for new types of emotional design; inspiration is found in online and offline features that illustrate the dialogue between humans and the world. She has exhibited in various festivals and galleries in Asia and Europe, and was awarded an honorary mention at the Ars Electronica for her project LED Eyelash. She is also a lecturer at Dankook University.

Keywords: emotional, fashion, wearable, media, fetishism, aesthetics

The LED Eyelash project originates from a simple question: Why do women want larger and more prominent eyes? Asian women tend to have a stronger need for bigger eyes as a standard of beauty, but relatively few of them are born with them naturally. Alternatives must be sought to make their eyes look prettier, i.e. larger – for example, a repertoire of skills such as putting on makeup and wearing jewelry. At the verge of

obsession, many women opt for plastic surgery in order to make their dream come true. Soomi calls this 'the fetish of big eyes'. LED Eyelash responds to this desire: It features an inclination sensor with mercury to turn it on or off, which follows the movements of the pupil and the eyelids. When you wear it and move your head, LED Eyelash will flicker accordingly. It is as simple as wearing false eyelashes and as easy to remove as a piece of jewelry. The LED Eyelash project was created at IDAS (International Design School for Advanced Studies), Hongik University in June 2007 using LEDs, an inclination sensor, battery, and headphone housing.

www.soomipark.com/entry/LEDeyelashes

Maison Martin Margiela
Line Artisanal

Margiela, the elusive Belgian designer who has never been photographed, is a 1980 graduate from the Royal Academy of Fine Arts in Antwerp, studying alongside the avant-garde fashion collective, the Antwerp Six. Since its founding in 1988, the Artisanal production – the transformation of fabrics, accessories, and clothing into new garments – has been a fundamental corner stone of Maison Martin Margiela's creative expression. Each garment or item is made or reworked totally by hand at the in-house atelier in Paris. The great amount of time dedicated to each piece and the scarcity of the vintage raw materials used means that the total number of editions produced of each piece is extremely limited. Each piece is therefore entirely unique.

Already in 1997, the visionary Maison Martin Margiela collaborated with a microbiologist to create a decorative decay effect by introducing bacteria that provide varying colors and textures.

Keywords: craftsmanship, vintage, re-appropriation, fashion

Mirror Structure Dress, S/S 2010
Double-face mirror Plexiglass is fastened together with big beads to create a garment structure open in the back. 14 hours were necessary for the creation in question, including: the preparation, the finishing, and the quality control but excluding the

research of raw material, technical control, necessary treatment (cleaning, softening, dying, etc.), and the fittings. The materials used were Plexiglass, jersey, and sequins.

Elastic Jacket, S/S 2008
Various widths and types of elastics are plaited directly on the dummy to make a jacket and a coat. The different types of elastics bring a particular color to each garment.

Wigs Jacket, A/W 2008-09
Blonde wigs are used to create a fur jacket.
51 hours were spent for its realization.

Record Dress, A/W 2008-09
A crêpe de chine dress is decorated with
33 and 45 rpm records. The records
have been cut, then shaped while warm
to mold to the shape of the body.

Balloon Jacket, A/W 2008-09
A jacket is made up of balloons with
different diameters. Thirty balloons are put
together by means of a twisting system.

Plastic Fur Jacket, S/S 2009
Plastic garment label fastenings cover
a leather straight jacket creating a
herringbone pattern fur. It required 42
hours and consists of 29,000 plastic garment
label fastenings and lambskin leather.

www.maisonmartinmargiela.com

Wigs Jacket

Record Dress

Balloon Jacket

Elastic Jacket

Plastic Fur Jacket

Mirror Structure Dress

Walter Van Beirendonck
Explicit / Take a Ride / Wonderland

The underlying story of a fashion collection can be further enhanced through accessorizing.

Walter Van Beirendonck studied fashion at the Royal Academy of Fine Arts in Antwerp. His first breakthrough was the British Designer Show, London in 1987 as part of The Antwerp Six (with Dirk Van Saene, Dries Van Noten, Dirk Bikkembergs, Ann Demeulemeester, and Marina Yee). Since 1983, he has been producing collections under the label Walter Van Beirendonck. Since 1985, Walter has been a teacher in the Fashion Department of the Royal Academy of Fine Arts in Antwerp.

Explicit

Take a Ride

Keywords: nature, technology, fashion, society

The collection Explicit from S/S 2009 deals with censorship. "We should have the right to know the real truth and experience real freedom." The collection did indeed seem to be inspired by nature: from blow-up prints of leaves and miniature scenes on hats and collars to green beards made out of leaves and other natural elements.

The collection Take a Ride from A/W 2010-11 is based on the idea of 'contrasts' and 'tensions' – namely, about the wars that divide men and are now, more than ever, affecting our society.

Robot Ken Wig

Robot Ken – Wig is from the collection
Wonderland from A/W 1996–97.
Complementing the plastic wig is a yellow
plastic device with buttons and a red antenna,
which can be attached to the arm with Velcro.

www.waltervanbeirendonck.com

81

CHAPTER 03

Scientific Couture

In the film The Man in the White Suit, directed by
Alexander Mackendrinck in 1951, the humble inventor
Sidney Stratton creates a miraculous fabric that will never
be dirty or worn out. Today's premises of nanotechnology
have been the idea for stories decades ago.

The merging of nature's creations with human inventions
brings forth new propositions for materials and forms. The
study of materials as a second skin has expanded to scientific
experiments. Explorations in biology often labeled as biomimicry
or biomimetics[1] examine nature as a resource for novel
developments. Janine Benyus describes biomimicry[2] as an emerging
discipline that seeks sustainable solutions by emulating nature's
designs and processes. Solar cells mimic leaves; experiments
with bacteria create bio-textiles. Objects that capture and
stimulate all our senses are designed using scientific data.

1   Seymour (2008a)

2   Benyus (2002)

There have been promising scientific advances applicable to design and fashion, and many visions will forge ahead through persistent exploration and interdisciplinary research. The subsequent projects explore the field in experiments that reappropriate existing substances or collaborations with scientists to create new materials. Others simply use natural resources to create engaging fashionable wearables.

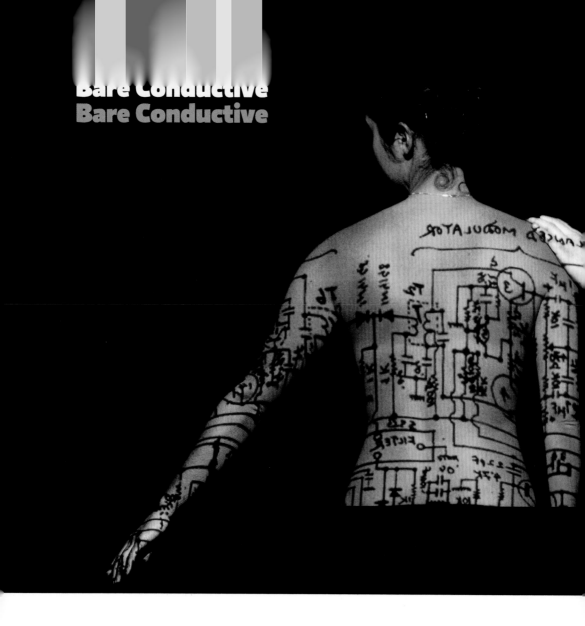

Bare Conductive
Bare Conductive

The implications of a conductive element applied directly onto the skin leaves room for many applications.

Bare, based in London, is the result of a graduate project at the Royal College of Art by Matt Johnson, Isabel Lizardi, Bibi Nelson, and Becky Pilditch.

Keywords: conductive, ink, body, skin, non-toxic, temporary

Bare is a skin safe conductive ink invented by four designers intent on creating a new space between wearable technologies and electronic

implants through direct application of electronic circuitry on the skin. Temporary, non-toxic, and water-soluble, Bare is composed of conductive carbon particles suspended in materials that are commonly found in food and cosmetic products, allowing for safe application on the skin with a brush, stamp, or spray. This unique material, first developed in 2009, has the potential to replace and augment existing technologies where wires are cumbersome or undesirable. Bare is currently being developed for use in medical devices, stand alone products, rapid prototyping, and larger-scale applications in the built environment.

www.bareconductive.com

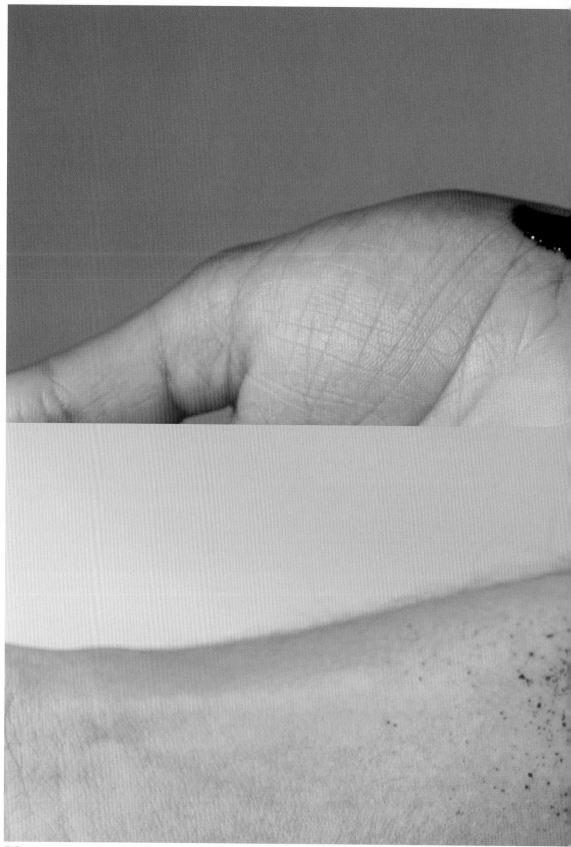

Donna Franklin & Gary Cass
Micro 'be' Project

Developments in bio-textiles using living organisms and explorations in biotechnology bring about new propositions.

The Australian artist Donna Franklin employs microbiology technologies in various collaborative projects on themes of commodity culture, identity, life, death, and empathy. In 2009, she exhibited in Biotech Art – Revisited at the Experimental Art Foundation, Adelaide, and Super Human at The Royal Melbourne Institute of Technology. Donna tutors at the School of Communications and Art, Edith Cowan University.

The Scottish/Australian Gary Cass is a scientific technician tutor in the Faculty of Natural and Agricultural Sciences at the Teaching Laboratories. Cass is a founding member of Bioalloy, an ongoing research endeavor into artistic cyborgian systems developed in the FNAS laboratories at the University of Western Australia (UWA). Cass' Bioalloy and the Body project with contemporary performer S. Chandrasekaran have been exhibited in the Venice Biennale 07 (fringe event), Documenta 07, and BEAP 07.

Keywords: bio-textiles, living microbes, fermentation, vivo culture

To modify the body through cosmetic surgery is an attempt to create material perfection and halt time on the basis of the 'ideal' human form. Micro 'be' aims to draw attention to the ethics of textile production and to change the current disassociation from the natural world by going beyond the current aseptic world and infiltrating the potential new future life-world of the everyday. The project was conducted at the Institute of Agriculture, UWA, from 2006 to 2010 in Perth, Australia. Living microbes (acetobacter bacteria) ferment wine into vinegar to produce a microbiological cellulose by-product (chemically similar to cotton). The use of wine intensifies the abject qualities of the fleshy material tied to the act of swallowing and consumption.

www.bioalloy.org

Lucy McRae
Peristaltic Skin Machine / Chlorophyll Skin / Metabolic Skin

Aesthetic studies involving the human body provoke new perspectives and enhancements.

Lucy McRae, based in Amsterdam, The Netherlands, bridges the worlds of fashion, technology, and the body. Trained as a classical ballerina and as an architect, her work is inherently preoccupied with the human body.

Keywords: skin, nature, low-tech

Peristaltic Skin Machine was commissioned by Transnatural, an exhibition in Amsterdam showcasing crossovers in nature and technology in 2010. The 2008 series of images titled Metabolic Skin were the original starting point (made from hardened panty hose and pneumatic hardware parts), an experiment merging low technology with high-tech materials on the body. The Peristaltic Skin Machine followed

Metabolic Skin

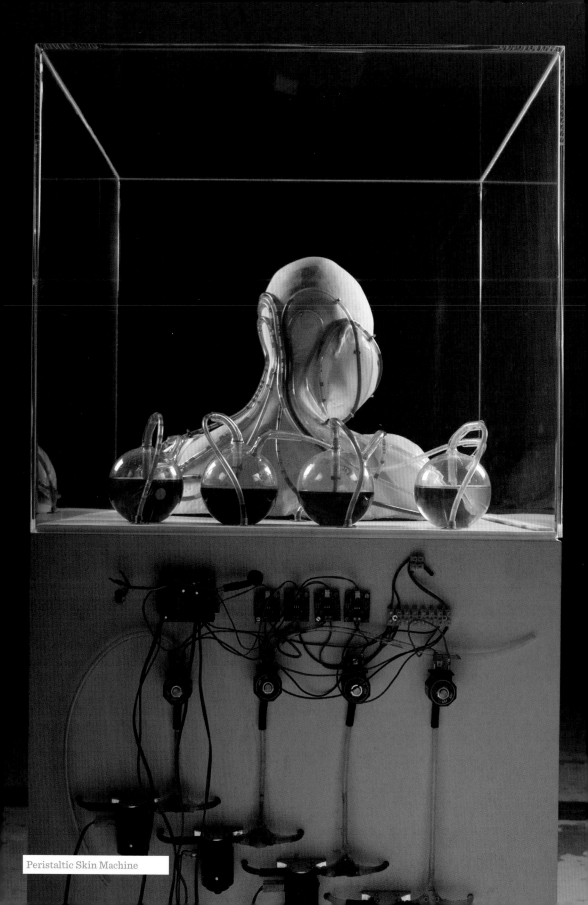

Peristaltic Skin Machine

Chlorophyll Skin

this series of images and was her first
opportunity to work with digital fabricator
Mike Pelletier. The intention was to create
a dynamic surface filled with liquid and
circulating air that wrapped the body. This
first sample is part of a bigger experiment
with water, liquids, and air on the body.

Chlorophyll Skin, a moving image project from
July 2009 with collaborator Mandy Smith,

investigates liquid, color, and absorption with
cotton ear buds. McRae's interdisciplinary
work is wholeheartedly about experimenting
with materials on the body and creating
images that provoke alternate worlds.

www.lucymcrae.net

93

Susanne Philippson
Cherrystone T-Shirt

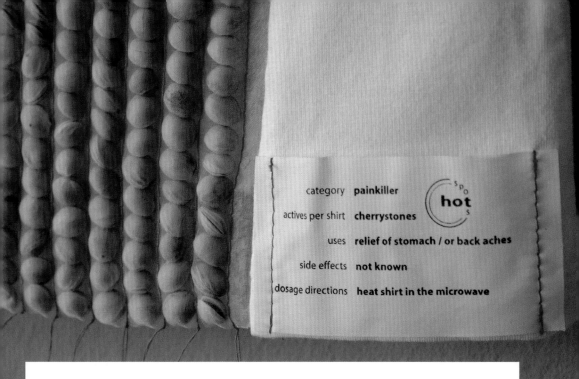

The combination of old traditions, natural ingredients, and modern technology is a strategy worth exploring more.

Susanne Philippson is a German lighting and furniture designer who chose to set up her business in Berlin after studies at Ravensbourne College in London and The Eindhoven Design Academy in the Netherlands. The idea of the Cherrystone T-Shirt was conceived while studying at the Design Academy in a department called Man and Well-Being, which perfectly suited her own personal interest. She sought to conceptually and functionally combine the healing power of a hot stone therapy with wearable clothing. The Cherrystone Shirt became part of the Droog Design Foundation Collection in 2002.

Keywords: microwavable, T-Shirt, heating, healing

The concept of the Cherrystone Shirt is based on an old principle of heating cushions that are filled with the pits of cherries to relieve pain through warmth. In the case of the Cherrystone T-Shirt, the pits are integrated into the garment itself – a wearable 'dry hot water bottle' for the stomach. One heats up the shirt for 1 minute at 600 watts in a microwave, or places the shirt in an oven until the cherrystones have heated up. Due to the naturally inherent moisture in the pits, the textile won't be affected. The stones release the heat to the wearer over a period of about 20 minutes. The shirt brings about well-being and soothes stomach aches. It can be machine washed at the standard 30°C (85°F).

www.susannephilippson.com

Suzanne Lee
BioCouture

*Research in biology and materials engineering
open new possibilities for a sustainable future.*

Suzanne Lee is a senior research fellow in fashion at Central Saint Martins College of Art & Design London and a creative consultant for London-based fashion brands. She is the author of the seminal book Fashioning The Future: Tomorrow's Wardrobe (Thames & Hudson 2005) and a recognized expert on how emergent technologies propose radical new innovations for the fashion industry. Lee consults, lectures, and exhibits her work internationally.

The team is comprised of research assistants Marion Piffaut and Nelly Ben Hayoun, scientific advisor Dr. David Hepworth, Cellucomp, and scientific collaborators: Prof. Alexander Bismarck, Prof. Paul Freemont, and Dr. Sakis Mantalaris (all Imperial College London).

Keywords: synthetic, biology, materials engineering, textile design

Director of the BioCouture research project since 2007, Suzanne Lee is pioneering a new field that unites fashion and textiles with the latest thinking from synthetic biology and materials engineering. BioCouture is a visionary and innovative research project with the aim to grow clothing. It unites fashion and textile design with bio and nanotechnologies for future sustainable fashion. Fashion designer Suzanne Lee works with scientists from the Centre for Synthetic Biology and the Department of Chemical Engineering at Imperial College London to produce a series of garments and products that are grown from bacterial-cellulose. BioCouture uses harmless bacteria to spin and simultaneously shape cellulose nano-fibers into a textile-like material. The sheet material is grown in a green tea solution and can be dried down to form a seamless shape or cut and sewn conventionally. It can also be colored and printed like normal fabric. The long-term aim is to grow seamless 3D-formed garments from vats of liquid. A key driver of contemporary textile innovation for fashion is the need to find new sustainable fibers and production techniques that contribute toward biodegradable garments and close the cycle of production, disposal, and reuse. Many of today's textiles are made from resource-hungry plant-based forms of cellulose such as cotton, hemp, wood, or manmade derivatives. Bacterial or microbial-cellulose, however, is produced when bacteria feed on a simple sugar solution – it is eco-friendly, biodegradable, and sustainable. BioCouture clothes can be composted with food or waste vegetation in the garden.

http://biocouture.posterous.com
www.biocouture.co.uk
www.tfrg.org.uk/node/13
www3.imperial.ac.uk/syntheticbiology
www3.imperial.ac.uk/polymersandcompositesengineering

Sonja Bäumel
(In)visible Membrane

The fusion of fashion design with scientific experimentation stimulates the creation of new metaphors and enables novel examinations of aesthetics.

After studying fashion in Vienna, Sonja Bäumel continued on to the master program at the Design Academy Eindhoven, The Netherlands. Her research work focuses work on art, (fashion) design, biology, and microbiology. Believing in symbiosis, networks, exchange, and individuality, her work approaches plants, animals, fungi, and even bacteria as equally respected partners in the search for solutions to global matters. Bäumel is based in Brussels, Belgium.

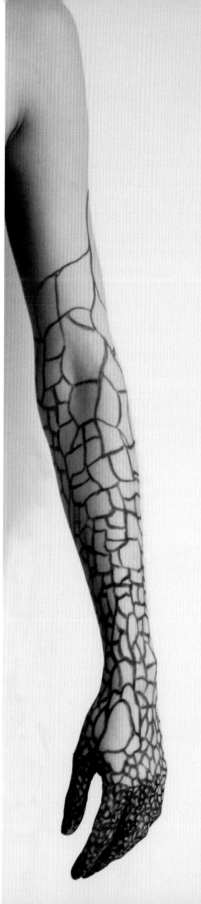

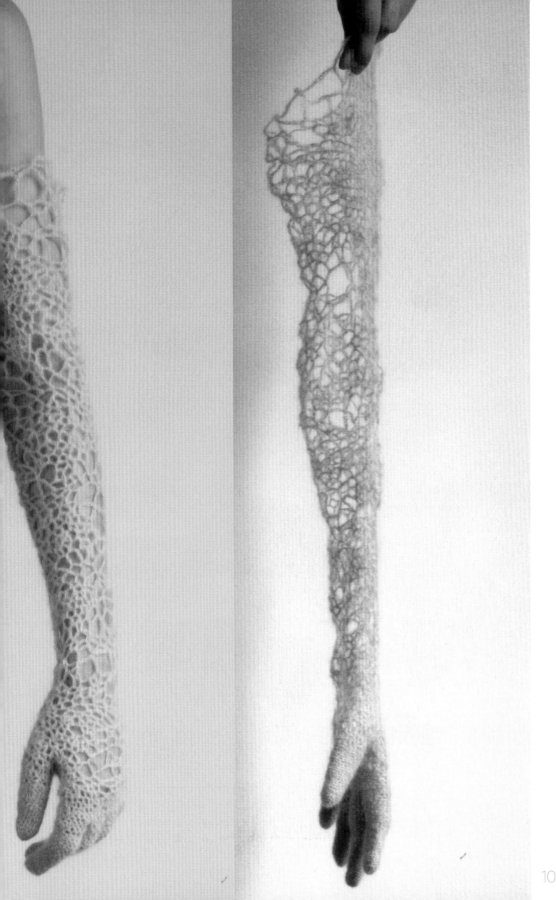

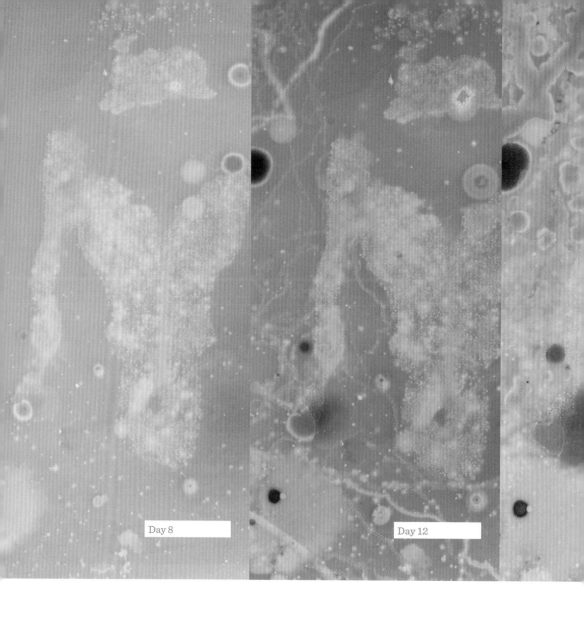

Day 8

Day 12

Keywords: biology, bacteria,
autonomous living, second skin

(In)visible Membrane consists of four projects
conducted at the Design Academy Eindhoven
in collaboration with the microbiology lab at
Wageningen University in The Netherlands
in 2009. 1. The Crocheted Membrane project
translates scientific data into crochet pieces
representing a design language in between
science and fashion design. The Invisible
Membrane would, for instance, react to the
body temperature via bacteria populations'
knowledge and to the local temperature. 2. In
the Invisible Membrane project, the scientific
data transfer and a visualization of individual
skin bacteria attempt to make people aware of
the fact that we are a hybrid, a super organism,
which obviously is only able to exist if the
different forms of life on the body cooperate.
A series of photos shows an oversized petri
dish (1100x750 mm) in which body-skin-
bacteria grow. 3. The Visible Membrane shows
the experiments with textiles and bacteria.

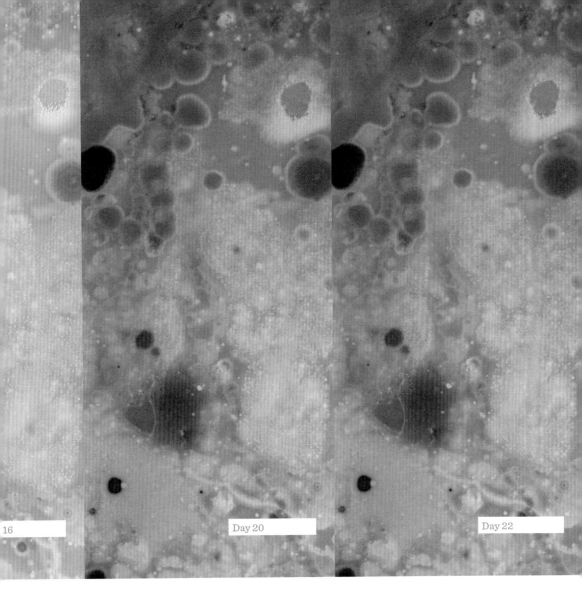

16   Day 20   Day 22

The experiments illustrate that bacteria react
to textile surfaces. 4. A film shows the author's
vision of the four layers of the (In)visible
Membrane and how, theoretically, this clothing
could transmute into different forms, colors, and
functions in relation to environmental changes.

Bäumel uses synthetic, natural, and
synthetic/natural textiles in combination
with agar and skin bacteria.

www.sonjabaeumel.at

Alexander Reeder, Cloud Design
S Ring

Alexander Reeder, based in Tokyo, Japan, continues to explore the fusion of human and digital through the design of interactive garments, perfume, and jewelry. He has a master's degree from New York University's Interactive Telecommunication Program and a BA in computer science and Japanese studies from Earlham College. Reeder collaborated with Carolanne Patterson (metalwork).

Keywords: perfume, jewelry, pheromone, interactive

The idea of a love perfume that causes another to fall instantly in love has existed for centuries. Historically, these scents have been sold with skillful banter, but today we utilize science to synthetically manufacture many pheromones the body produces. S Ring brings style and control to scented jewelry by releasing a pheromone-laced perfume into

The human sense of scent has yet to be explored extensively in fashionable technology.

the air surrounding its wearer. The wearer can playfully direct the scent with their hand, perhaps toward a desirable other. While we may not be able to accurately affect the behavior of others with pheromones today, this will change in the future. Imagine a pheromone mix concocted after the analysis of an other's DNA. Without their knowing, their behavior could be unconsciously influenced. S Ring was produced in New York in 2009 using

silver, glass, piezo ceramic, feather, custom circuit, wire, and a rechargeable battery.

http://artandprogram.com

CHAPTER 04

The Epidermis as Metaphor

The epidermis, or the skin, is our principle communicator of emotional and physical states. It communicates through blushing, sweating, and variations in tension and temperature. These localized variants can be extended through the use of sensor and actuator technologies. Sensors are able to detect signals from the skin and actuators, and in turn can produce certain types of visual, sonic, or haptic output. Reciprocally, this output can appeal to our physiological and psychological senses. "Helmut Lang's fashion often showed skin at the expense of figure. It played upon the theme of fabric as second skin."[1] Smart materials and textiles as our second skin can stimulate our senses, whether they are conductive textile coatings or electronic plastics on the surface of the garment.

In the movie Ultraviolet from 2006, which is set in the 21st century, the character played by Milla Jovovich can instantly change the color of her outfit. In a commercial for PS3 by Sony from 2009, people wear T-shirts that 'play' scenes from movies. Currently, such dynamic displays are visually augmented and gratify certain aspirations, but are not yet a reality. However, already in 1956, Atsuko Tanaka, an avant-garde artist from Japan, designed the Electronic Dress made of blinking colorful light bulbs using light to

---

1   Warwick, Cavallaro (2001:136)

attract people's attention. Today, LEDs are the medium of choice to gain attraction as exemplified in Bono's Laser Stage Suit by Moritz Waldemeyer.

In my future vision, visual data is dynamically generated on the surface of the garment. It enables a real-time interaction and customization by the wearer. Garments become animated canvases.

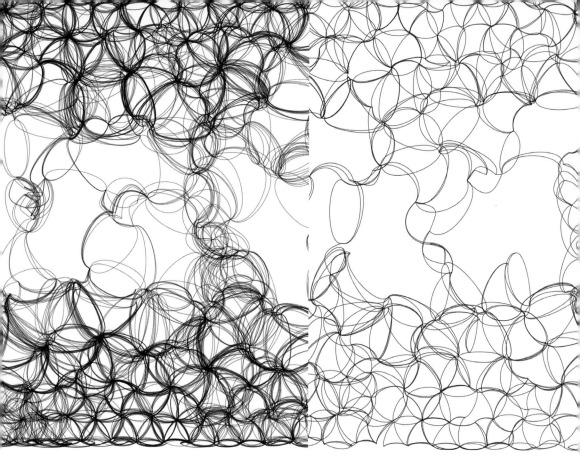

Cait and Casey Reas
Tissue Collection /
Generated Network Scarf Series

The use of generative software for the creation of real-time dynamic patterns on the surface of a garment unveils many visionary applications.

Generated Network Scarf Series

1 of 1 is an independent design studio by Cait Reas that synthesizes fashion and art into one-of-a-kind apparel, made to order in Los Angeles. Each signed and numbered piece results from her collaboration with a commissioned artist. Cait works with the artist's imagery and applies it to the body. C.E.B. Reas is an artist who focuses on defining processes and translating them into images. He is a professor in the Department of Design Media Arts at the University of California, Los Angeles. In 2001, he co-founded Processing, a programming environment for visual artists and designers. Reas' software has been featured in numerous solo and group exhibitions at museums and galleries in the United States, Europe, and Asia.

Keywords: generative software, digital printing, moving images

The Tissue Collection was created with C.E.B. Reas in 2007. The Tissue software reveals the movements of autonomous software machines. Each line in the image represents the path of each machine's movement as it responds to stimuli in its environment. People interact with the software by positioning the stimuli on the screen. Through exploring different positions of the stimuli, an understanding of the total system emerges from the subtle relations between the simple input and the resulting fluid visual output. Cait used a digital printing technique to apply the Tissue images to fabric. Still images in the collection are taken from software animations.

The Protean Image tennis dress (not
shown) was created in collaboration
with C.E.B. Reas, Serena Williams, and
Nike for the Australian Open in 2009.

The Generated Network Scarf Series was
designed with C.E.B. Reas in 2009-10.
He created a software to explore network
relationships with which Cait Reas
experimented and developed a series of
images that were printed onto fabric. Cait
was interested in the relationship between
digital networks and traditional textile
techniques such as lace and knitting. Each
scarf in the series is completely unique.

http://1of1studio.com
http://reas.com/iperimage.php?section=wor
ks&view=&work=tissue_collection&id=0

Tissue Collection

CuteCircuit
Galaxy Dress

*Illuminating garments are the predecessors
of fully dynamic textile-based displays.*

CuteCircuit, based in London, is a fashion company that designs wearable technology products, innovative intelligent clothing that integrates new functionalities into fashion through the use of smart textiles and microelectronics. They combine wearable and telecommunication technology and create emotionally rich experiences for users in the fashion, sport, and communication industries.

*Keywords: LED fabric, luminous,
lightweight, smart surface*

The Galaxy Dress was the centerpiece of the Fast Forward: Inventing the Future exhibit at the Museum of Science and Industry in Chicago in 2008. In celebration of its 75 years, the museum commissioned the Galaxy Dress for their permanent collection.

Embroidered with 24,000 full color LEDs, the Galaxy Dress provides a spectacular and mesmerizing effect and is the largest wearable display in the world. It uses the smallest full color LEDs, which are flat like paper and measure only 2x2 mm. The circuits are extra-thin, flexible, and hand embroidered on a layer of silk in a way that gives it stretch, so the LED fabric can move like normal fabric with lightness and fluidity. Additional materials include silk chiffon, silk organza, silk taffeta, and Swarovski crystals.

www.cutecircuit.com/products/galaxydress

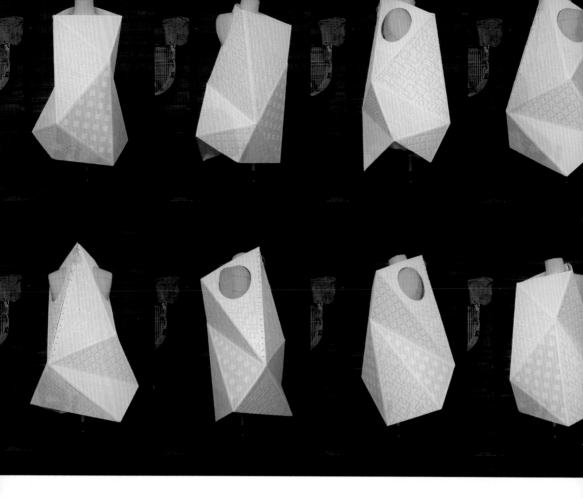

Jum Nakao
01

*Projections on the surface of a garment in a performance
setting fuels imagination beyond the possible.*

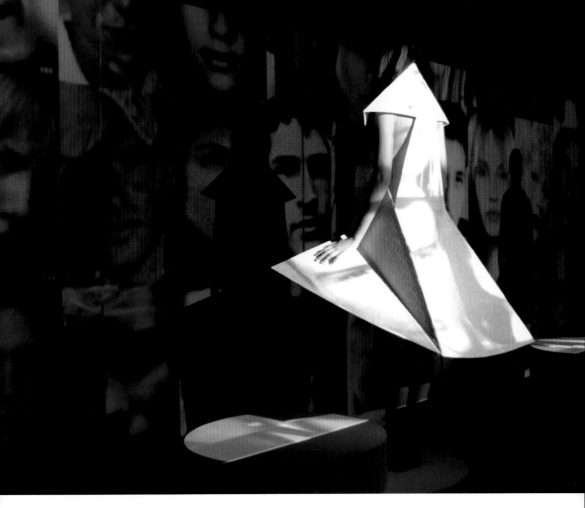

Jum Nakao is a fashion designer and a creative director based in São Paulo, Brazil, who was invited by Du Pont in 2002 to be the partner fashion designer in the Hotel Lycra International Project. In 2004, Nike established the premium line Jum Nakao for Nike. He has exhibited internationally at Galeries Lafayette in Paris, Oscar Niemeyer Museum in Brazil, and the New Dowse Museum in New Zealand. Jum holds numerous lectures and workshops around the world about his creative process. Nakao has collaborated with Fernanda Yamamoto, Silvana Marcondes, and Pop Design.

Keywords: distortion, projection, dress, surface

Jum was invited by OI, a Brazilian telecommunications company, to create a dress as a surface for the projection of Brazilian fashion history. As Brazilian culture is very fragmented, an amalgam of different origins, he designed a polygonal dress surface to distort the images – there is never one point of view, rather many angles as it is in Brazil. The structure is made of polyester tubes connected with silicone strings, and the surfaces are polycarbonate overlaid with wallpaper textures. The performance was held in a tent on a historical bridge in São Paulo on October 24, 2008.

www.jumnakao.com.br

Kerri Wallace
Garment I-D: Fashioned for Performance™

*Explorations in smart textile design represent
a testbed, and the viable results afford
potential realization by the industry.*

Kerri Wallace is a textile designer whose work concentrates on the research and development of new materials, existing and emerging technologies, smart textiles, and investigative approaches in printed textile design. She has a master's in Design for Textile Futures from Central Saint Martins College of Art & Design. In 2006, Kerri received an Arts and Humanities Research Council Research Preparation Master's Award to support her work on responsive printed textiles (Motion Response Sportswear). Kerri is currently a senior lecturer in printed textiles at De Montfort University (UK) and research associate for the Textile Futures Research Group, University of the Arts London.

Keywords: fiber, inkjet, laser etching, digital imaging, textiles

Garment-ID, launched in 2008, is an interplay between cloth fabrication and printed textile

design using non-conventional materials and approaches to challenge preconceptions and traditions in clothing. While form, fiber, or style categorize some garments, a generic name or a single word can describe or associate others. Printing processes such as dye sublimation inkjet printing, laser etching, and screen-printing are employed to probe new patterning interpretations of digital imaging, re-surfacing, and trompe-l'oeil impressions for printed textiles and functional garment design. Considerations include environmental factors such as the use of recycled and recyclable fibers, mono-materials, and digital inkjet printing methods.

www.kerriwallace.com

Zane Berzina
E-Static Shadows

This artistic translation of electrostatics manifests the potential of harvesting energy from our immediate surroundings.

Dr. Zane Berzina, born in Riga, Latvia, works at the intersection of the realms of science, technology, design, art, crafts, and culture. Her practice and research involves responsive environments, soft technologies, membrane systems, and biomimetic methods. Zane collaborates with electronic engineers, material scientists, and biologists, synthesizing various cultural and scientific concepts, methodologies, and processes that link new technologies and smart and industrial materials with more traditional textiles approaches. Since 2008, Zane has been a professor for conceptual development of materials and surfaces at the Art College Weißensee Berlin, Germany. She is also an associate of the Goldsmiths Digital Studios, London, and a co-founder and director of electronic-text+textiles (e-t+t) in Riga, Latvia.

Collaborators were Prof. Janis Jefferies, Constance Howard Resource and Research Centre in Textiles, Goldsmiths, University of London; Jackson Tan, Insquare Lab, London; TITV – Textile Research Institute Thuringia-Vogtland, Germany; Dr. Tim Blackwell, Goldsmiths Digital Studios, London; and Dr. Natalie Stingelin-Stutzmann, Queen Mary University of London. The research project E-Static Shadows was funded by the Arts and Humanities Research Council (2007–09).

Keywords: e-textiles, electrostatics, responsive environments, static mirror, LEDs

The research project E-Static Shadows explores the speculative and poetic potential of the static electricity surrounding our interactions in built environments. The study investigates how this electrostatic energy can be translated into other types of energy for the development of responsive textile systems. These systems are capable of detecting, processing, and displaying electrostatic charges as dynamic audio-visual patterns on the surface of the e-textile, which effectively functions like a static mirror. These poetic translations, embedded in the soft medium of cloth, provoke a higher awareness of the electrostatic waves in our habitat and initiate playful interactions between the viewer(s) and the space. E-Static was produced using conductive threads, LEDs, transistors, and woven circuitry.

www.zaneberzina.com/e-staticshadows.htm

Moondial & Wendy&Jim
SUN No 1

Storytelling via interactivity on the surface of a garment possesses great appeal.

Moondial is a fashionable wearable technology studio and lab focusing on design, fashion, and mobile and wearable technologies based in New York and Austria. Moondial develops fashionable wearable products and consults on fashionable technology worldwide. Hermann Fankhauser and Helga Schania founded the Viennese fashion label Wendy&Jim in 1999. They started working together when they were students at the University of Applied Arts Vienna in the class of Helmut Lang. Since then, they show their prêt-à-porter fashion in Paris and create performances

and installations in international museums and galleries around the world.

Keywords: photochromic, dynamic surface, storytelling, fashion, Tencel

The surface of the garment lends itself to the display of interactive storytelling. The conversion of a static interface into a dynamic one by the simple natural power of the sun is the basis of SUN. Moondial and Wendy&Jim launched a limited edition of this new series of shirts at the Ars Electronica Festival in September 2009. SUN uses the shirt as a canvas to tell a story and the sun as the switch to turn on the graphic. As such the static graphic becomes an interactive story.

www.moondial.com/sun

Vincent Leclerc, ESKI
Flip Deck

The visual surfaces of boards (skateboards, snowboards, surfboards) stir emotions and transform into dynamic (customized) interfaces.

Vincent Leclerc mixes inductors and bread dough in the hope of one day creating a crusty 802.11 baguette. He spends most of his time steering electrons at ESKI, stitching circuits at XS Labs, and teaching physical computing at Concordia University in Montreal, Canada.

Keywords: skateboard, light, kinetic

The Flip Deck is a skateboard equipped with an organic matrix of LEDs controlled by an 802.15.4 radio and was developed together with Pierre-Yves Lavoie in May 2009. The deck allows its users to display various abstract animations that evoke motion and speed. Its patterns are based on xylem, the cellular structure present in many plants and trees. This cellular structure is responsible for transporting water and nutrients through the plant's vascular system. The electronic circuit that controls the flow of light on the deck employs a similar transport structure consisting of flip-flop gates. The entire circuitry is embedded in the plywood of the skateboard.

http://vincentleclerc.com
http://vincentleclerc.com/flip
http://eskistudio.com
www.transistordesign.com/expo5
http://design.concordia.ca

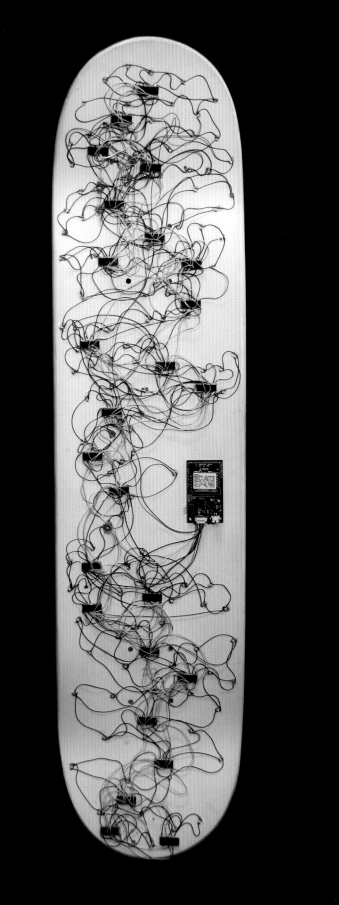

CHAPTER 05

Material Explorations

In the 1960s, with the advent of the moon landing, fashion designers like Paco Rabanne, André Courrèges, and Rudi Gernreich seem to have brought space to earth. Paco Rabanne's fashion experiments produced tiny metal, vinyl, and plastic link dresses. His explorations with these outré materials proved influential in the innovation of high-tech fabrics and garment construction. André Courrèges' Couture Future collection in 1967 and Birth of the Second Skin collection in 1969 marked a use of materials not yet adopted by the fashion industry.

With the appearance of smart textiles and materials like conductive textiles, shape-memory alloys, and electronic plastics, innovative interfaces for fashionable wearables are created. Fashion design as 'the art of creating for the body' gains in importance. The construction of technically enhanced garments requires specialized expertise that resides in the fashion industry. The worlds of fashion, science, and technology are rapidly merging.

Advances in material science and reappropriations of existing materials through design will lead to visionary examples. The diverse projects presented here, from the use of smart textiles to nanotechnology, encourage further development of materials and applications. Additionally, some projects reveal the power of existing materials, or simply nature as an inspiring resource.

Bart Hess & Lucy McRae
Grow on you #1 / Exploded View / Germination / Hook and Eye / Evolution / Grow on you #2

The manipulation of the human form through simple materials prompts the rethinking of beauty and stresses the significance of technology.

→ Biography Bart Hess on page 66, Lucy McRae on page 90.

Keywords: body, performance, low-tech, beauty, nature

The projects were created in Rotterdam, The Netherlands in 2008.

Grow on you #1 uses dish washing liquid and food color. The foam was 'mass-produced' by using huge buckets and a handheld blender. This photo shoot captured an unexpected moment as the liquid didn't stand still.

Exploded View creates an explosion on the body made only from paper. Paper was cut up in all different shapes and angles, and the pieces that sculpted the skin best were glued to the body starting from one point and working in a spiral outwards.

For Germination, a pantyhose is stuffed with sawdust and grass seed. In the first shoot, the textile was dry and draped over the body. The second shot shows it after 8 days of watering. It is part human, part animal, and self-replicating. Grown at different densities

and viscosity, it lives and breathes with us.

Hooks and Eyes are glued to the face with skin glue and are brought into tension with cotton thread. This mechanical movement brought forth a series of unusual facial expressions. The landscape of the face is redefined by moving the cheeks or emphasizing the lips, creating a low-tech version of plastic surgery.

Evolution suggests that men and women are becoming more similar. Balloons stuffed in pantyhose emphasize a muscular silhouette.

Grow on you #2 uses blue felt balls glued to the skin. It explores the possibility of growing color, shape, and texture from the pores of the skin.

http://lucyandbart.blogspot.com

Exploded View

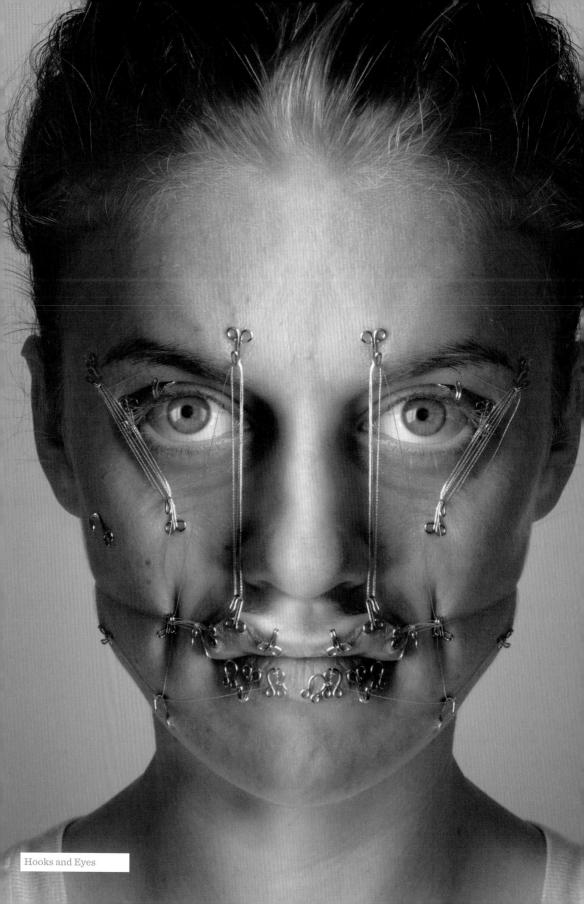

Hooks and Eyes

Germination Day 1

Germination Day 8

Grow on you #1

Grow on you #2

Gluejeans
Gluejeans #1

The application of successful new methods in the production of traditional garments encourages further investigations.

The designer duo Gerrit Uittenbogaard and Natasja Martens left the sewing machine for what it was. In 2008, they discovered that gluing instead of sewing actually works, even for a conventional, steady pair of jeans. Gluejeans is handmade in the Netherlands and is available in a limited edition at Droog. The duo won a Dutch Design Award for Gluejeans and has been nominated for the Audi Design Award as well as the Fashion Award.

Keywords: glue, jeans, material

Jeans as we know them have changed. Unlike your traditional pair of jeans, Gerrit and Natasja's innovative 'gluejeans' haven't been stitched, but are glued together from top to bottom showing a distinctive play of glue lines. The ultra strong glue has been pigmented to obtain different colors. The result is a pair of jeans that looks familiar like your old-fashioned jeans but, upon closer look, is totally different. It has a minimal, raw look but is still comfortable, and the dry denim used will only get more beautiful the longer you use it. Gluejeans were extensively tested for over 2 years to ensure the quality and durability of the product.

www.gluejeans.com

Ross Lovegrove
Seed of Love

Fiber and fabric investigations, and the creation of design objects that convey the benefits of such materials are inspiration to further explore the relationships between creators and suppliers.

Ross Lovegrove is an expert in ergonomy, a creator of designs that attempt to stir users' emotions. The materials and manufacturing techniques Lovegrove chooses are invariably leading-edge and follow the guidelines prescribed by Green Design, which calls for ecological awareness in the entire design process and more durable products. Born in Cardiff, Wales, in 1958, Lovegrove studied industrial design at Manchester Polytechnic and at the Royal College of Art in London. In 1986, he set up a London-based joint practice with Julian Brown before founding his own in 1990, Studio X. He created Seed of Love with Kenya Hara for Tokyo Fiber '09.

Keywords: Senseware, triaxial woven fabric, backpack, organic design

Seed of Love is an ultra lightweight backpack with an organic shape, which utilizes the properties of triaxial woven fabric. Unlike conventional textiles that warp and weft intersecting at 90 degrees, triaxial woven fabric employs three threads intersecting each other at 60 degrees in a reticulate arrangement. Structures ideal for tracing dynamic surface changes in three dimensions emerge. A material that has been used for aerospace appliances in space development programs is applied here to a backpack.

The complex projections and depressions stabilize the form, contributing to its three-dimensional strength and shape stability.

"Created hand in hand with digital software, the Seed of Love layers structure over structure to extend the emotions of aesthetics outward from the inward and into an object that communicates desire and subtle seduction: white intimacy, white lace, white grace, and silent awareness of love like clouds and air."

www.rosslovegrove.com

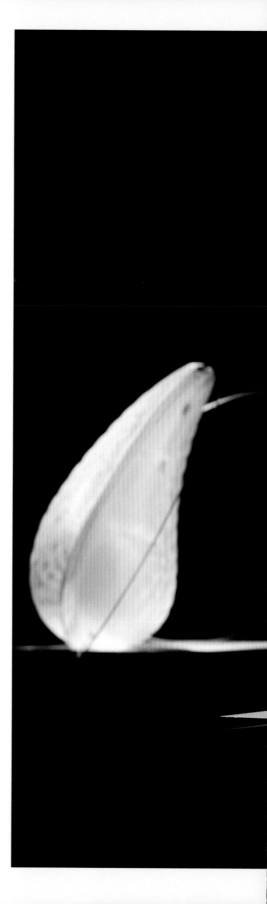

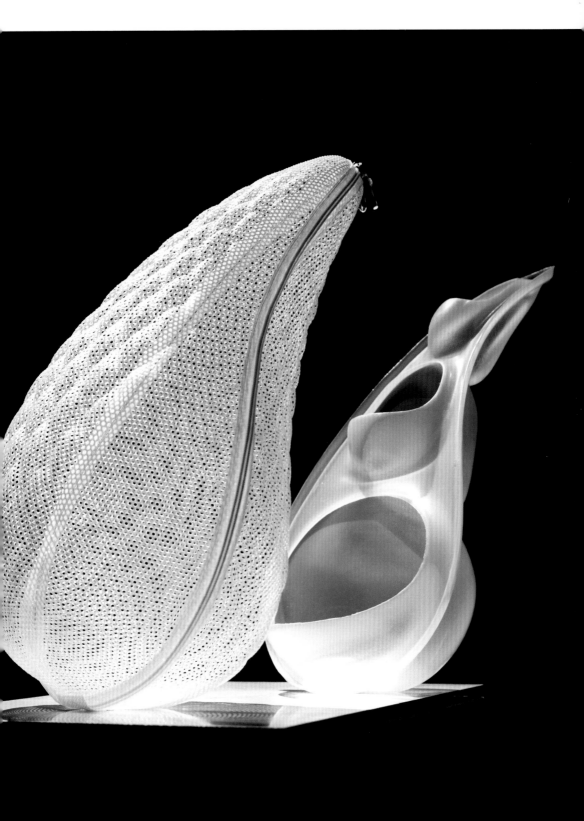

Caleo-Tex

Grado Zero Espace
Caleo-Tex / ReLIGHT

Innovations in material engineering lead to the creation of new products that respond to an expressed need by the end user.

Grado Zero Espace is a company specialized in design, innovation, and technology. Their mission is to develop new materials and technologies for industry with the aim of improving quality of life. The company acts in partnership with many industrial branches and research fields including the European Space Agency. Their innovative materials and ideas are finding myriad applications in fibers, fabrics, composite textile structures, extreme sport equipment, and safety equipment.

Keywords: nanoparticles, impregnation, electro-luminescent, light

Caleo-Tex is a textile finishing treatment based on carbon nanoparticles able to confer conductive properties to natural fibers and fabrics. The result is a cotton warmer than wool when properly powered. The special impregnation process – simple, fast, low cost, and potentially applicable at an industrial level on cotton yarns and fabrics – can also have

reLIGHT

wearable applications. Impregnation of yarns and/or fabrics in a bath containing a suitable dispersion of CNTs (carbon nanotubes) and further dyeing procedures create a proper chemical bond between the textile material and the nanoparticles, and guarantees a very good workability and aesthetic effect of the final product. This technique was also used to introduce molecules into the yarn that are able to react with albumin, which is present in human blood. The aim is to detect and monitor, through appropriate conductivity measurements, the physiological health of people wearing the treated cotton garment. Commercial applications of Caleo-Tex commenced in 2010.

reLIGHT is a new generation light source based on electro-luminescent technology. reLIGHT is a soft shining cape with physical-mechanical properties that make it lightweight, foldable, and durable. Thanks to its unique light emission – diffuse, uniform, fascinating – reLIGHT is well-suited for wide and continuous surfaces, while its flexibility makes packaging, transportation, and installation easy and fast, minimizing size and overall dimensions. It meets the latest product and interior design requirements and opens a range of possible applications: from fashion to packaging, from automobiles and boats to the aerospace sector.

www.gzespace.com

Fraunhofer IZM
Klight, The Interactive Dress

Collaborations between research institutes, commercial entities, and universities breed innovative applications of new technologies and materials.

Since 2001, Fraunhofer IZM has been working on the integration of electronics into textiles. The focus of the institute is on assembly and reliability. In 2009, Fraunhofer IZM launched TexLab, where the corresponding competence and equipment are concentrated. The collaborative and interdisciplinary work style at TexLab has led to a diverse range of projects in the fields of automobile interiors, medical science, fashion design, interior design, and logistics. The team consists of Christian Dils, Mareike Michel, Manuel Seckel, and René Vieroth.

Keywords: stretchable circuit board, interactive dress, STELLA (EU project)

Klight is an interactive dress that communicates with its environment by translating the body's movement into a corresponding light pattern. Textile-integrated LEDs fade in and out according to the intensity of movement. To achieve this effect, a novel substrate technology has been used: Developed in the framework of the European integrated project STELLA, the stretchable circuit board (SCB) is based on a thermoplastic polyurethane foil and can be easily integrated into textiles through lamination. The pattern of the body's movement is detected by an acceleration sensor and processed by a microcontroller, which is used to control the illumination pattern of the LED array. Klight is comprised of textile: night-blue cotton cambric fabric; an electronic system: ATmega 644P microcontroller, two 16-channel, 12-bit PWM LED controllers and a 3-axis acceleration sensor, 32 warm-white LEDs, lithium-polymer battery with 1Ah capacity; substrate: 30x40 cm large stretchable circuit board; and interconnection: 40 cm long textile ribbon with stretchable wiring and snap fasteners.

www.stretchable-circuits.com
www.fraunhofer.izm.de
www.stella-project.de
www.mareikemichel.de

nendo
Blown Fabric

Traditional craft and art forms, with their many design propositions, are a valuable source for inspiration to promote meaningful creations with smart textiles and novel materials.

nendo / Oki Sato received a master's in architecture from Waseda University, Tokyo, and set up the nendo Tokyo office. In 2005, nendo established an office in Milan. In 2009, Ghost Stories was shown at the Museum of Arts and Design and the Friedman Benda Gallery in New York. His works are in collections of The Museum of Modern Art, Museum of Arts and Design, Cooper-Hewitt | National Design Museum (all in New York), Musée des Arts décoratifs, Paris, The Montreal Museum of Fine Arts, and the Design Museum Holon, Israel.

Keywords: synthetic fiber technology, light, lanterns, Senseware

nendo created Blown Fabric for the Tokyo Fiber '09 Senseware, an exhibition about the possibilities of new materials developed with Japanese synthetic fiber technology. 'Smash' is a specialized long-fiber non-woven polyester that can be manipulated into different forms through hot press forming technology. Its thermoplastic, light, and rip-proof qualities – and the beautiful glow when light passes through it – led to a design for lighting fixtures in the style of vernacular Japanese chochin paper lanterns. With Smash's unique properties, it could be shaped like blown glass into a seamless one-piece lantern. As Smash changes form when the interior temperature rises above 80°C, low-heat LED bulbs were mounted in machined aluminum sockets that double as a heat-sink to maintain a low interior temperature.

www.nendo.jp/en/works/
detail.php?y=2009&t=134

V2_Institute for Unstable Media
Intimacy

The use of an architectural material and the psychological effects of its transparency illustrate how new materials can be applied to body architecture.

V2_ has a long history of supporting, presenting, publishing on, and (co)developing wearable technology in collaboration with artists and universities. While in the past these projects predominantly consisted of handheld devices and other body-extending hardware, V2_ has in recent years shifted its focus to fashion. V2_Lab has created various tools and applications that are now available for innovative uses in new artistic projects. By making these technologies available under creative commons licenses, V2_Lab aims to fulfill the role of a central hub in contemporary wearable technology artistic research and development (aRt&D). The collective included Daan Roosegaarde and Maartje Dijkstra.

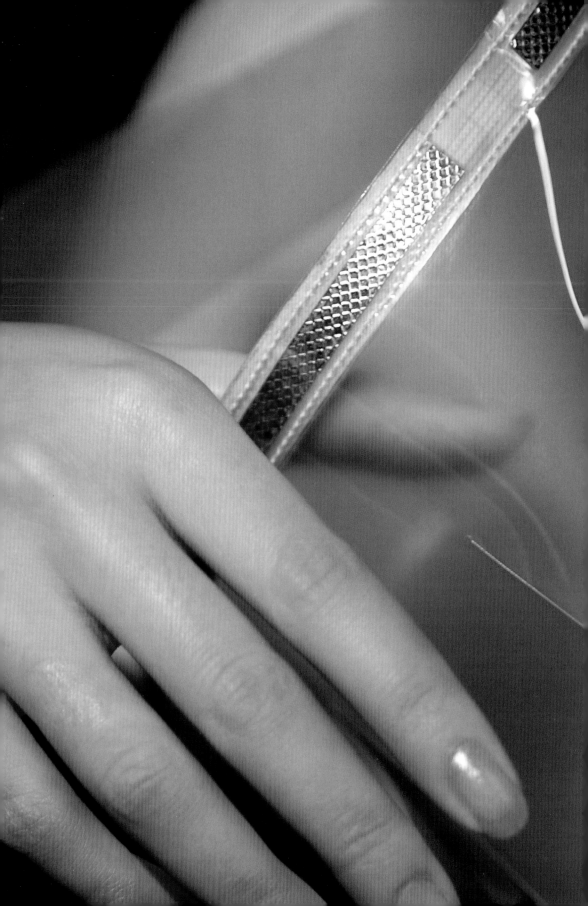

Keywords: smart foil, transparency,
wireless, sensors, intimacy, fashion

Intimacy is a project that combines the worlds
of fashion, wearable technology, and the
electronic arts, while exploring the relation
between technology and intimacy in our
contemporary technology-driven society. The
project consists of high-tech garments made
with wireless, interactive technologies and
smart foils that can become transparent. It is
constructed of PDLC foil (Polymer Dispersed
Liquid Crystal), copper tape, and sensors.
The distance between a spectator and the
garments determines the garments' level of
transparency, creating an intimate experience
and a sensual play of disclosure. As an ultimate
statement on exposure, the dress responds
to flashlight: For example, if a photographer
takes a picture of the dress, it becomes
fully see-through in the blink of an eye.
Intimacy was produced at V2_Lab and Studio
Roosegaarde, Rotterdam, The Netherlands
from September to December 2009.

www.v2.nl/lab/projects/intimacy
www.studioroosegaarde.net

Azuma Makoto
Leaf Man

In 2002, Azuma Makoto opened his first flower business, which has now expanded into the haute couture flower shop JARDINS des FLEURS in Tokyo. Parallel, his first gallery exhibition in New York led to international exposure, and in 2005 he designed the Christmas window display at the Colette boutique in Paris with critical acclaim. In 2009, he displayed his work at the Tokyo Fiber '09 Senseware and also designed a line of shoes and clothing for adidas Originals called the PLANTS PACK. In spring 2010, Azuma presented his new work Armored Pine at his solo exhibition in POLA Museum Annex. In all of his work, Azuma explores the mystical forms and ultimate beauty inherent in flowers and plants, translating it into artistic expression to give them the reverence they deserve and to raise awareness about botany.

Keywords: humans, green, dreams, nature, plants, Senseware

"I don't know who s/he is.
s/he has nothing but name.
s/he never moves
s/he never talks
s/he is just standing 20 m ahead.

An inspiring installation exhibits the beauty and functionality inherent in nature and stimulates further exploration of the power of biology.

s/he might be a friend.
s/he might be myself.
s/he might be a monster.
the only thing I know is
the sense of distance 20 m from the Leaf Man
is equivalent to that between plants
and me when I think about them
not too close, not too far
I would look at him/her just like I saw a tree.
if the distance between creativity
and me appears in this sense,
it means I'm really addicted to the plants
however it might be good for
me to meet him/her

no creation is worth while
unless I'm addicted."

Makota used the following plants: alocasia odora, asparagus asparagoides, asparagus pella, cast-iron plant, dracaena sanderiana, dypsis lutescens, Ellen Danica, erect sword fern, leatherleaf fern, and monstera.

www.azumamakoto.com

CHAPTER 06

Transparent Sustainability

Transparent sustainability announces the entire life cycle of a product, reveals social interventions, exemplifies the environmental and health implications, finds solutions for the smart exploration of energy on and through the body, and applies novel materials for sustainable housing. The promise of sustainability is multifaceted. An example is the Repair Manifesto by Platform21.[1] I prefer the notion of transparency in the creation of an awareness that will hopefully lead to change. The endeavor of making a Parsons[2] Sourcemap[3] to trace a product's life cycle provides transparency and enables designers to have tangible resources when designing a product.

Today, sustainability in fashionable technology is often directly correlated with materials or energy harvesting. Despite their low efficiency, solar panels are the current alternative energy source of choice. Eclipse announced a collaboration with Samsung in January 2010, which marks another step in the advances of fashionable technology in a larger consumer market, benefiting from expertise in construction, sourcing, and

---

1   www.platform21.nl

2   www.newschool.edu/parsons

3   www.sourcemap.org

branding. In spring 2010, Elle magazine organized a competition to create solar bags by renowned fashion designers.

The skin as a natural climate regulating surface[4] and biomembrane is explored by architects in the design of an ideal passive house. The advances in sustainable material technology are blurring the delineators between fashion and architecture, both being disciplines that construct a shell with its many properties. These developments in the creation of new surfaces, energy solutions, climate control, etc. bring together scientists of all disciplines with designers. Nature is inherently the most important influence on human life and shall become a blueprint for the design of sustainable objects. Nature's vast resources need to be examined for their implications on design and manufacturing.

4   Klooster (2009)

Elena Corchera
LFLECT /
Solar Street Lights

The call for sustainability often correlates with local production and is examined particularly when prototypes require specialized craftsmanship.

Elena Corchera, founder of Lost Values, envisions a future where technology helps us to become more human and less machine-like. Her lifestyle products embrace craft and tradition as well as new technologies and innovative materials. Elena studied fine arts in Spain and Germany, and completed the Textile Futures Masters at Central Saint Martins in London, UK. With interest in the power fashion has to reach people, she decided to explore wearable technology as a research associate at MIT Media Lab Europe. Determined to make sustainability one of the major driving forces in her work and after various international exhibitions, publications, and awards, Elena joined Distance Lab as a senior researcher. In 2008, Lost Values, based in London, was formed with their support.

LFLECT

Solar Street Lights

Keywords: smart, fashion, sustainable, technology, textiles, solar

LFLECT is a collection that resulted from investigating the lifestyles of city cyclists. When cycling is no longer a sport but part of your everyday life in the city, you want to be safe without compromising on style. Could reflective products be desirable, only visible for cars, and at the same time stylish? LFLECT was awarded the Best Use of Materials Blueprint Award in 2009 at 100% Design London. Inspired by vintage clothing, the collection started with lace trimming that you could buy per meter and stitch into your own garments; today, there is also knitwear, pompoms, lace scarves, bows, socks, etc. LFLECT is locally produced in London and the highlands of Scotland using lace, Scottish wool, and organic cotton.

Inspired by Shoefiti, the act of hanging shoes from the electrical cables in cities, Solar Street Lights makes street style an eco style by turning your old sneakers into solar lights. It is a kit that you can attach to your old shoes. Lost Values encourages renewable energies. Solar Street Lights is made of solar cells, waterproof circuitry, and high intensity LEDs.

www.lostvalues.com
www.lflect.com

Kate Hartman
Glacier Human Communication Techniques

The project draws attention to nature's enormous influence of nature on the earth's ecosystem by 'communicating' with disappearing glaciers.

Kate Hartman is an artist, researcher, and educator whose work spans the fields of physical computing, wearable electronics, and conceptual art. She is the co-creator of Botanicalls, a system that allows thirsty plants to place phone calls for human help, and the Lilypad XBee, a sewable radio transceiver that enables your clothing to talk. Her work has been exhibited internationally and has been featured by the New York Times, BBC World Service, NPR (National Public Radio), and in the book Fashionable Technology. Hartman is currently based in Toronto, Canada, where she is the assistant professor of Wearable & Mobile Technology at the Ontario College of Art & Design.

Keywords: reflective, material, sound, communication

Produced in Banff, Canada in 2009, the glacier embracing suit is made of heat reflective material that acts as insulation for humans and the glacier. When lying down, the human is insulated from the cold of the glacier and the heat of the human does not make the glacier melt. The glacier embracing suit can be seen as a glacier communication device. "Conceptually, I am exploring the possible ins and outs of how we (humans) and glaciers might communicate, considering both explicit acts such as talking and listening, and more implicit ways of relating such as 'body' language and non-verbal communication. I am attempting to approach these studies from both the human and glacier perspectives. Practically and technically, I'm building prototypes – from physical constructions to electronic sensing systems – to see what data and which transmission methods can provide the best understanding."

www.katehartman.com

Mary Huang & Jennifer Kay
Dandelion

Mary Huang is a designer from California who works at the intersection of communication design, fashion, code, and electronics. She completed her BA degree in Design | Media Arts at University of California, Los Angeles and MA at the Copenhagen Institute for Interaction Design (CIID), Denmark. Jennifer Kay studied product design in Glasgow and is now exploring interaction design at CIID. User research has always been integral to Jennifer's process, and she loves nothing more than delving deep into an experience

to find opportunities. She has a keen interest in the latent potential of technology, especially within public space. Advisors were David Gauthier and Di Mainstone.

Keywords: wind power, windmills, energy-generating, sustainable, recycling

Inspired by the topic of climate change, Dandelion explores ideas of personal, mobile power generation and kinetics. It was produced at the CIID, Denmark in December

This project creates awareness for natural and renewable energy using windmills as design inspiration.

2009. Dandelion is a wearable that captures energy from wind and human movement. It is a structure of miniature windmills that embraces the wearer. It is fashion that creates an interface between nature, technology, and people. The windmills turn when walking or standing outside on a windy day. Small individual power generating circuits transfer the rotational energy into usable voltage. In this prototype, the power generated turns on white LEDs, but the energy could be used to power mobile devices or stored

for later use. Additionally, Dandelion was made with 99% salvaged materials using recycled wood, a DC motor, transistor, LEDs, inductor, and recycled paper.

www.rhymeandreasoncreative.com

XS Labs
Captain Electric & Battery Boy

The possibilities of harvesting energy from the human body are exemplified in an artistic project that allows for playful explorations.

XS Labs, based in Montreal, Canada, develops enabling technologies and methods in the form of soft electronic circuits and composite fibers, and explores the expressive potential of soft reactive structures. Many of their electronic textile innovations are informed by the technical and cultural history of textile production but use a range of materials with different electro-mechanical properties. They involve the soft, playful, and magical aspects of materials to better adapt to the contours of the human body and the complexities of human needs and desires. Their approach often engages subtle elements of the absurd, the perverse, and the transgressive. Narratives are constructed that involve dark humor and romanticism as a way to drive design innovation. This integrative approach allows them to construct composite textiles with complex functionality and sophisticated behaviors. Collaborators were Marc Beaulieu, Anne-Marie Laflamme, Gaia Orain, and Vincent Leclerc.

Keywords: parasitic power,
e-textiles, reactive garments

Captain Electric, produced in 2009, is a collection of three electronic garments – Itchy, Sticky, and Stiff – that both passively harness energy from the body and actively allow for power generation by the user. Reflecting fashion's historic relationship between discomfort and style, the dresses restrict and reshape the body in order to produce sufficient energy to fuel themselves and actuate light and sound events on the body. They conceptually reference safety apparel and personal protection as well as our fears of natural disasters and other states of emergency, personal phobias, anxieties, and paranoia. Using inductive generators, kinetic energy from the human body is converted into electric energy and stored within a power cell integrated into the garments. Rather than attempting to conceal the generators and their operation, they are overtly integrated into the garment concept and design.

http://captain-electric.net

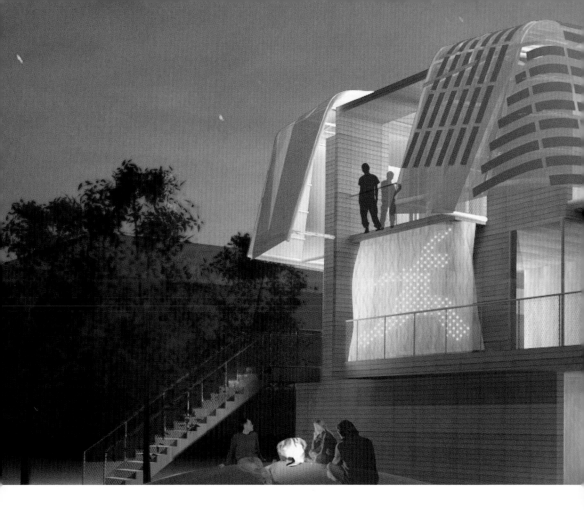

KVA Kennedy & Violich Architecture
IBA Soft House

*Architects can be vanguards by using novel materials
to achieve 'softness' and sustainable solutions.*

Founded in 1988 by principals Sheila Kennedy and Frano Violich, Kennedy & Violich Architecture, Ltd. (KVA) is a Boston-based interdisciplinary design practice that explores new relationships between architecture, technology, and emerging public needs. KVA recently developed FLAP - an adaptable solar textile kit that integrates flexible photovoltaics and solid state lighting for use in areas without electricity.

Keywords: sustainable energy, nanomaterials, solar, smart architecture

The Soft House is an integrated sustainable energy concept, combining a carbon-negative wood construction system with the innovative use of flexible solar nanomaterials. A textile roof cladding harvests energy and provides a climate buffer that provides shade in summer and limits heat loss in winter. The flexible solar cladding opens to provide views, harvest sunlight for energy, and create a dynamically changing façade. Clean energy from the roof is distributed via the smart building network and a simple system of movable smart curtains. These provide a low voltage ring that optimizes energy usage for household electronics and intelligent LED lighting. The Soft House will be constructed in Hamburg, Germany between 2010 and 2012.

www.kvarch.net

CHAPTER 07

Woven Interface

Technology and fashion are not as distant as it might first seem. The thread-up and thread-down of the weaving process correspond to the binary logic of 0 and 1 of computer circuitry. Ada Augusta, Countess of Lovelace, born in 1815, wrote notes on the 'Analytical Engine' by Charles Babbage, detailing how it could be programmed to compute a complex sequence of numbers. The input (programs and data) was to be provided to the machine via punched cards, a method used at the time to direct mechanical looms such as the Jacquard loom.

Today, digital Jacquard looms can translate digital data into complex woven structures, and the advances in digital technology for knitting, embroidery, or printing enable new processes in the creation of textiles. However, the cost of these machines and the lack of availability for tinkerers breed open source applications like OSLOOM, which will become a DIY electromechanical thread-controlled loom inspired by MIT's FabLab[1]. The MIT FabLab has successfully brought open source hardware and software to explorers of all kind, thus enabling new practices and alliances.

---

1   http://fab.cba.mit.edu

Technology can be a part of the actual textile (e.g. smart textiles), a tool for their creation (e.g. the software CAD), or used to manipulate the input (e.g. using wearable technologies). The diverse applications of technology provide fascinating solutions in the creation of textiles and are documented in the subsequent projects.

Anke Loh
Urban Identities/Transnational Spaces

The exploration of data and its translation into fashion and textile design through digital technology produces new styles.

Anke Loh studied fashion at the Royal Academy of Fine Arts in Antwerp, earning a BFA in 1998 and an MFA in 1999, and was a visiting fellow at the Research Centre for Fashion, the Body and Material Cultures, London College of Fashion, where she collaborated with Sandy Black and Reiner Rockel in 2010. Anke Loh's fashion design has been shown internationally. She investigates new ways of analyzing how society is organized and renegotiates new boundaries for contemporary fashion.

Keywords: transnational spaces, society, technology, fashion

Urban Identities/Transnational Spaces is a new interpretation of knitwear garments, which was presented during NY fashion week in February 2010. Colorful video stills (Video Spin Cycle, 2008) taken from Luminex dresses in motion (optical fiber dresses with different color LEDs) were put into a computer software of a knitting machine. The goal was to achieve a layered textile that translates the light movement into a ready to wear and contemporary garment. The collection was produced in New York and Chicago, USA with the Stoll Fashion & Technology Center .

www.ankeloh.net
www.fashion-body-materialcultures.org
http://fashion.stoll.com

Trikoton
Trikoton

For customized designs, ranging from purely aesthetic creations to specific functionality, input generated by the human body will play a greater role in the future.

Founded in Berlin, Germany in 2009 by designers Magdalena Kohler, Hanna Wiesener, and computer scientist Hannes Nützmann, Trikoton works with local manufacturers, bringing together traditional and new technologies to ensure high quality products for conscious consumers.

Keywords: knitting, sound, personalization

How does it feel when your sweater becomes a medium of your own voice? Trikoton transfers voices into clothes. The frequency bands of an audio message are converted into binary codes for knitting patterns. Together with a German knitting company, Trikoton created a parametrical knitting web application to produce fashion pieces via the Internet – unique like the human voice.

www.trikoton.com

Maggie Orth
Barcode Man

The Barcode Man is an elaboration of previous projects and presents the evolving body of work of a pioneer in this field.

Maggie Orth is a 2000 USArtist Target Fellow and holds a PhD from the MIT Media Lab, where she created pioneering works in electronic textiles and fashion. Her company, International Fashion Machines, based in Seattle, USA, created early e-textile products, including the POM POM Dimmer. Her current pieces include programmable color change textiles (woven electronic circuits, thermochromic inks, drive electronics) and interactive textile sensors and light pieces. Her work juxtaposes the feminine and the masculine, the decorative and the functional, and explores the intersection of physical form, active materials, and computation.

Keywords: woven, electronic, textile, thermochromatic, dynamic

Barcode Man from 2008 is a 72 pixel, 54" by 54", hand woven, evolving, color change textile. Highly conductive yarns are woven in the warp and resistive yarns in the weft. Plain weave electrically connects them on the selvedges, which are coated with silver ink, cut to create different color change areas, and connected to drive electronics. Software sends current to the areas, heating the resistive yarns and changing the color of the ink. The color change effect is reflective (does not light up); the software creates new sequences and patterns. Over time, the color change effect is permanently burned into the surface of the textile, creating a new artwork which reflects the mark of software on traditionally static art materials. Applied materials are cotton, stainless and polyester steel yarn, silver wrapped yarn, silver ink, thermochromic ink, water based screen ink, wire, wood, and electronics software.

www.maggieorth.com

Sarah Kettley
Aeolia

Dr. Sarah Kettley (TansleyShakeshaft Design), based in Southwell, UK, is a jeweler and researcher working between the fields of wearable computing, interaction design, and contemporary craft. Her projects, often collaborative, are primarily concerned with socially created networks of people and things, human creative processes of meaning and use, and distributed, shared, and co-created experience. She exhibits and publishes regularly in the UK and internationally, and lectures in design at Nottingham Trent University in the UK. Collaborators were Philip Breedon, Amanda Briggs-Goode, Martha Glazzard (knit), Tina Downes (embroidery), Nigel Marshall (weave), Karen Harrigan (fit), Yann Seznec (sound), and Peter Gregson (cello).

This project was generously supported by an Alt-w R&D award administered by New Media Scotland, a Crafts Bursary from the Scottish Arts Council, a research fellowship at Nottingham Trent University, and technical textiles funding from the Worshipful Company of Drapers.

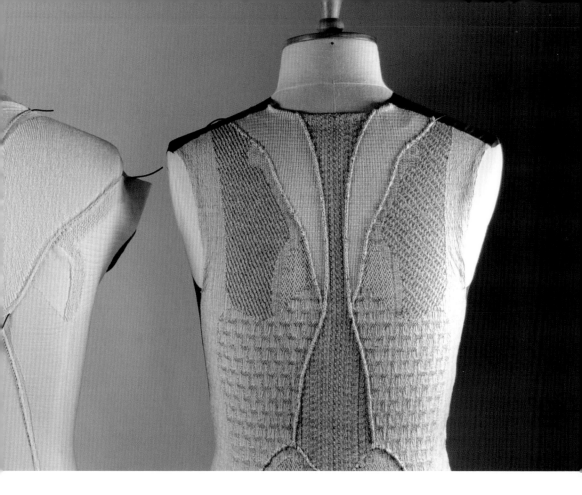

A stylish design and contextualization is necessary to make on-body sensing an everyday item.

Keywords: stretch sensing, knit sensors, aesthetic functionality, wearable technology

Aeolia addresses the design process of wearable technologies, focusing on the interdisciplinary development of aesthetically considered technical textiles for on-body sensing. Two strands of the project have emerged dealing with the integration of stretch sensing into garment forms. The backs utilize specialist textile knowledge to embed carbonized rubber cords in highly fitted forms, while the cello garment (not shown) is a working model for the potential of knitted stretch sensing in musical performance. Developed in Edinburgh, UK between 2009 and 2010, Aeolia is made of textiles, yarns, carbonized rubber, and custom electronics.

www.sarahkettleydesign.co.uk/sarahkettley/ aeolia_new_media_scotland_alt-w_ntu_textile_ interface_stretch_sensor_sarah_kettley_.html

Linda Kostowki & Mashallah Design
T-Shirt Issue

*New methodologies in fashion design lead to
new forms and aesthetics. The use of actual body
data adds a personal layer to the creation.*

Linda Kostowski was born 1980 in Poland and raised in Berlin, where she studies experimental fashion design at the University of the Arts. Hande Akcayli was born 1974 in Turkey and studied fashion in Moscow and Istanbul. Hande co-founded Mashallah Design in 2007 with Murat Kocyigit, who was born 1974 in Germany and studied product design at the College of Fine Arts in Hamburg and at the University of the Arts in Berlin. The project grew out of a first time collaboration in 2008.

*Keywords: 3D scanning, laser
cutter, body, pattern*

Three people are portrayed digitally by scanning their bodies. The output of this scan is a 3D file; the resolution is defined by the amount of polygons, similar to pixels in a bitmap graphic. The 3D data is turned into 2D sewing patterns via the unfolding function, a common tool in industrial design to make paper models. The single fabric pieces and the inner interface that defines the edges are cut out with a laser cutter. This unfolding process fundamentally changes the aesthetics of the garment because contrary to ordinary pattern construction methods, orientations like center front or the shape of an armhole are irrelevant.

www.the-t-shirt-issue.com
www.mashallahdesign-lacaptas.com
www.realfakewatches.com

CHAPTER 08

Context as Prerequisite

Fashionable technology objects need to be contextualized to be commercially and artistically successful. The context conveys the story. It allows for the intent of the product to be communicated by the creative practitioner and comprehended by the consumer. Applying a contextual analysis as designers of fashionable wearables, we can define the degree of computation needed, ranging from non-computation to fully computational[1]. The object's story also defines the degree of functionality needed, from expressive and aesthetically striking to a primarily purposeful design. These explorations inform the brand definition and its attributes. A lead user[2] might reappropriate the product and create a new form of utilization, which could be considered the first advance in a human-centered design process.

Context is essential for any story, whether an artistic exploration, a critical intervention, or a product. As part of 80+1[3], the Romanian artist Flaviu Moldovan contributed the Microblogging Suit for an Industrial Worker. It is a prototype communications suit that endows industrial workers with a voice they can use to issue communiqués about their job and everyday life. The repetitive

---

1   Seymour (2008a:13)

2   Hippel (2005)

3   www.80plus1.org

actions from three workers in Romania were verbalized into live tweets. The story of this project is simple yet striking and shows the impact of contextualization and the use of the actual workwear.

To create human-centered design solutions rather than merely conducting explorations is a vision shared by many designers and will lead to competently constructed fashionable technology objects. The subsequent projectspropose innovative forms of use and, at the same time, reveal the power of storytelling.

adidas
miCoach

Monitoring vital signs is a growing market niche for body and health conscious individuals.

adidas is headquartered in Herzogenaurach, Germany. The adidas Innovation Team (ait) consists of diverse experts trained in industrial design, mechanical and electronic engineering, product development, and biomechanics. The textile sensor was developed by Textronics, which was purchased by adidas in 2008.

Keywords: heart rate, monitor, stride sensor, textile sensor, sports

By tracking your heart rate, pace, distance, and stride rate, the miCoach interactive training system instructs you to speed up or slow down for the perfect training. The miCoach Pacer communicates wirelessly with your Heart Rate Monitor and Stride Sensor to record your workout stats. During each workout, you can choose to hear elapsed time, calories, heart rate, among other information. Afterwards, the stats can be synchronized with the website to track your improvement. miCoach was designed in Portland, OR, USA and launched as a consumer product in 2010. It is produced in Malaysia and composed of plastics, FR4 circuit boards, integrated circuits, batteries, headphone jacks, and a fabric strap.

www.micoach.com

Fibretronic
HEATwear™ / i-Lume

Easy to integrate and price conscious, OEM solutions are essential for the rapidly growing fashionable technology market.

Fibretronic, based in Hong Kong, China, is a leading developer, manufacturer, and supplier of soft electronic technologies and components designed specifically for application in clothing and soft goods. Fibretronic's product range includes keypads, switches, sensors, heating systems, lighting products, textile data cables, and communications accessories.

Keywords: wearable electronics, technical lighting, flexible LED devices, textile heating

HEAT*wear*™ is a textile based heating system designed for technical apparel applications. The system consists of a patent-pending textile heating element that can be manufactured in custom shapes and sizes to suit a variety of garment products. The textile heating panel is a laminated construction comprising of conductive fibers, PU films, and warp knitted fabrics. A textile cable power bus connects the heating panel to an EVA Li-ion battery pack that provides up to 9 hours of heating. The heating panel is controlled by a Fibretronic i-Lume LED switch that can be sewn into the garment in an easily accessible place. HEAT*wear*™ was launched in 2010.

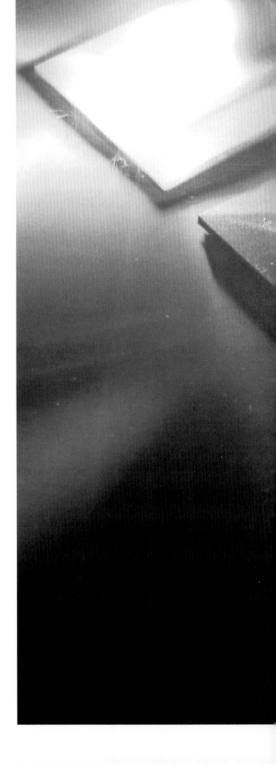

i-Lume is Fibretronic's branded range of wearable lighting systems, integrating high brightness LEDs and switches into flexible rubber formats suited for application in apparels. They are designed for technical purposes such as increased night visibility and torch/nightlight functions. The i-Lume torch module can be added to outerwear to provide a unique and easily accessible torchlight. The i-Lume spotlight button provides a high visibility safety light and can also be used as an on/off indictor switch to operate other wearable technologies such as heating systems. i-Lume was launched in 2009.

www.fibretronic.com/products/heatwear
www.fibretronic.com/products/ilume

i-Lume

Liquid Image
Summit Series Snow Camera Goggle / Wide Angle Scuba Series

The automatic capturing and transfer of visual data is of great interest to science and can be applied to activities of all kind.

Summit Series Snow Camera Goggle

Liquid Image, LLC is a manufacturer of cameras, electronics, toys, and games that targets sports and outdoor activities with a focus on sports technology and point of view cameras. It is headquartered in Sacramento, USA with an international office in Hong Kong, China.

Keywords: goggle, digital camera, sports, underwater, snow

The Summit Series Snow Camera Goggle integrates a wide angle lens digital camera. The hands free unit has a camera and video mode: Simply turn on the camera, choose the mode, and press the shutter button. Large buttons on the right side of the frame allow for greater dexterity while wearing gloves. The new Liquid Image Wide Angle Scuba Series HD322 Camera Mask features a 135-degree wide-angle lens and HD 720P video. The mask has lever style buttons along the upper right corner of the frame, which are easy to press while wearing diving gloves, and similar camera and video modes like the Snow Goggle. In both goggles LED lights inside the mask indicate the mode to the user. The goggles were launched as products in 2010.

www.liquidimageco.com

Wide Angle Scuba Series

Philips
DirectLife

Active healthcare monitoring will have many implications for an aging, technology savvy population who will want to age comfortably and with style.

Royal Philips Electronics of The Netherlands, headquartered in Eindhoven, is a diversified health and well-being company, focused on improving people's lives through timely innovations.

Keywords: monitoring, activity, healthcare, lifestyle

DirectLife, launched in 2009, records a person's daily movements via a discreet, wearable, state-of-the-art Activity Monitor, which tracks both the duration and intensity of a user's daily activity using 3D digital accelerometer technology. The monitor is small, lightweight, and waterproof. Information is then easily transferred in one simple step via USB to a personal web page that keeps track of progress against both daily targets and longer-term goals. It is the use of all three mechanisms of support together – monitoring, measuring, and motivating through a personal coach – which Philips believes will lead to healthier everyday decisions and a sustained active lifestyle.

www.directlife.philips.com

Rip Curl
H-Bomb

The ability to perform activities in extreme weather conditions has implications far beyond sports.

Rip Curl is an Australian surf company that has been making wetsuits since it was founded in 1969. It is headquartered in Torquay, Australia.

Keywords: surfing, heating, carbon fiber coils

Launched in 2009 as a consumer product, Rib Curl advertises the H-Bomb as the world's first power heated wetsuit. The temperature is controlled via three different heat settings located on a switch panel, using color-coding to indicate the setting. Heating elements are positioned on the back of the H-Bomb suit with batteries in internal pockets in the lower area. Rip Curl notes that the major challenge was to build a suit that included batteries, electronics, and heating elements with minimal impact on the flexibility and comfort of the wearer. The suit introduces the E3 neoprene, a thinner neoprene that offsets the weight of the heating components. The heating elements are 'free flying' carbon fiber coils, configured to attain maximum stretch in the back panel where they are located.

www.ripcurl.com

Biodevices
VitalJacket

Real-time, long distance medical diagnosis through wearable monitoring has merits far beyond the healthcare industry.

Biodevices, SA is a spin-off from IEETA (Institute of Electronics and Telematics Engineering / University of Aveiro, Portugal) with the mission to develop, commercialize, and export biomedical engineering solutions for medical diagnosis support. Biodevices is based in Espinho, Portugal. Project collaborators are IEETA and Petratex (Paços de Ferreira, Portugal).

Keywords: long-term ECG, medical diagnosis, monitoring

In development since 2008, VitalJacket® uses No-sew technology, a new technique for seamless garments where the details are joined with special glues. The Vital Jacket® HWM is a heart wave monitor that continuously stores data up to 72 hours. The product consists of a T-Shirt, a small hardware box that is placed in a pocket, and disposable electrodes.

www.vitaljacket.com
www.biodevices.pt
www.ieeta.pt
www.petratex.com

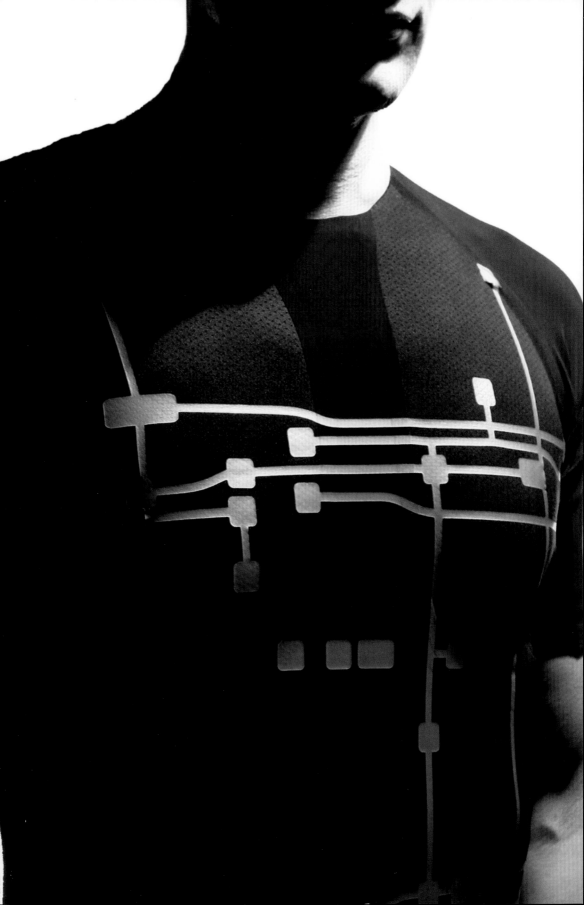

Adam Harvey, AH Projects
Camoflash: The Anti-Paparazzi Clutch

The project contextualizes a societal phenomenon and the issue of privacy, and proposes a fashionable solution.

Adam Harvey is a multidisciplinary designer living in Brooklyn , New York. The foundation of his work is visual communication and interactive design. During his residency in New York University's Interactive Telecommunications Program, Adam studied physical computing, which led to the prototype for his anti-paparazzi clutch. Currently, Adam is exploring the potentials for fashion and corporal technologies to enhance personal privacy.

The core project team members are Adam Harvey, John Luciani (electronics), Yelena Konovalova (fashion design consultant), and David Goetz (industrial design consultant). Contributors are Heather Knight (technical consultant and prototype development), Zach Eveland (wearable technology instructor and technical consultant), and Tom Igoe (physical computing instructor).

Keywords : privacy, camera, flash, light, camouflage

In the hands of an artist, a camera is a machine of expression; in the hands of paparazzi, it becomes a means of suppression.

The accessibility of digital photography has launched a new era of camera culture, putting a premium on privacy and making the ability to hide a luxury for some, a necessity for others. By emitting an overexposing pulse of light in response to a camera flash, Camoflash™ protects its user from unwanted flash photography. Currently in final stages of development, the Camoflash™ system will be introduced in 2010 as a limited edition anti-paparazzi clutch bag consisting of high brightness LEDs, LED optics, batteries, insulation, custom hardware, software and circuitry.

http://ahprojects.com/exhibitions/anti-paparazzi
www.wiblocks.com
www.eyedazzlerdesign.com
www.amalgam.com
http://marilymonrobot.com
www.blacklabel-development.com
http://tigoe.net

Jayne Wallace
Personhood

Creating digital jewelry for human relationships and exploratory storytelling can only be described as technology for humanity.

Jayne is a digital jeweler who works in a hybrid research group of computer scientists, artists, electronic engineers, and theorists. Her focus is the enrichment of what is at the heart of jewelry (personal significance, connections to meaningful experiences, people, and places) through the infusion of digital technologies. Her recent research led to digital jewelry that advocates an empathic engagement with people who live with memory loss. The items are also tangible and reassuring aids for people with dementia and their families, supporting their understanding of who they are and what they have experienced. The project was developed at Newcastle University, UK between 2008 and 2010. The project team also included Prof. Patrick Olivier, James Thomas, Daniel Jackson, Guy Schofield, David Green, and John Shearer.

Keywords: digital jewelry, participatory research, memory loss

"The project was developed through in-depth, co-creative research with a married couple, Gillian and John, one of whom is living with dementia. Gillian used to own many beautiful dresses. Many years ago, the dresses had been put in a pile to be thrown away, but John couldn't bear to part with them completely because they held such strong memories, so he cut remnants of fabric from each dress. We wanted to give Gillian a way to wear her dresses again and to nurture her understanding of herself in relation to who she is now and has been. The dress brooch can hold each remnant of fabric within it and be used with the jewelry box to record and play back sound. We wanted to give the couple ways to capture the memories the dresses relate to for future recollection, comfort, and reflection." The project was in part funded by the Arts Council England, UK and supported by the Alzheimer's Society, UK and the Institute for Ageing and Health. The project Personhood was constructed using walnut, rubber, velvet, silver, stainless steel, an RFID reader, microphone, speakers, and electronics.

www.digitaljewellery.com
www.side.ac.uk

Kits & DIY

The DIY movement has many facets and is important for product development exploration and prototyping. The arrival of many kits is a testament of the need for tools to create cheap and rather quick prototypes whether at universities or in professional studios.

The comprehensive list of materials, methods, and tools in my previous book is extended here with kits and DIY resources.

Blogs

Craft
www.craftzine.com

DIY Solar
http://voltaicsystems.com/diy

Fashionable Technology
www.fashionabletechnology.org

Fashioning tech
www.fashioningtech.com

iHeartSwitch
www.iheartswitch.com

Instructables
www.instructables.com

Kobakant
www.kobakant.at/DIY

Make Magazine
http://blog.makezine.com

MIT FabLab
http://fab.cba.mit.edu

OSLOOM
www.osloom.org

Tech D.I.Y.
www.techdiy.blogspot.com

Online materials libraries

CNMAT Resource Library
http://cnmat.berkeley.edu/resources

Material Connexion
www.materialconnexion.com

Transmaterial
http://transmaterial.net

Kits and material sourcing

Aniogmagic
www.aniomagic.com

All Electronics
www.allelectronics.com

Plug and Wear
www.plugandwear.com

Sparkfun
www.sparkfun.com

Watterott
www.watterott.com

Ayah Bdeir
littleBits

littleBits is a growing library of circuits made easy by tiny magnets! All logic and circuitry is pre-engineered, so you can play with electronics without knowing electronics. The library is open source and fosters a community of amateur inventors. littleBits was supported by Eyebeam and developed in collaboration with Jie Qi, Ted Ullrich, and Luma Eldin (design).

http://littlebits.cc

5050Ltd
Modules

The modules collection is a series
of electronic building blocks for
creating systems that sense and
respond. 5050Ltd originally created
the modulesfor the rapid development
of new wearable applications.

www.5050ltd.com/modules

Leah Buechley
Lilypad Arduino

The LilyPad Arduino is a set of sewable electronic components with conductive thread that lets you build your own soft, interactive fashion. It includes LilyPad sensors, actuators, power supplies, etc. The LilyPad Arduino was designed and developed with SparkFun Electronics.

http://web.media.mit.edu/~leah/LilyPad

Fibretronic
CONNECTEDwear™

CONNECTED*wear*™ is a unique
range of plug-and-play controls for
personal electronics such as iPod,
iPhone, MP3 players, mobile phones,
and music phones. The integrated
textile components (e.g. the keypads
and joysticks) are sold separately from
the electronics modules, enabling
designers to integrate this wearable
technology into their own projects.

www.connectedwear.com

Inspirations

Many of the artists, designers, and researchers in this book haved shared the inspirations for their projects. I want to thank all contributors for the sheer amount of references provided as it will enable meaningful research and further exploration of many of the topics touched upon in this book.

Websites, blogs

www.boingboing.com
www.core77.com
www.craftscouncil.org.uk
www.dezeen.com
www.ecouterre.com
www.engadget.com
www.fashiontech.com
www.form.net.au
www.gizmodo.com
www.interactivearchitecture.org
www.livraison.se
www.materialbeliefs.com
www.newscientist.com
www.notcouture.com
www.PDNOnline.com
www.riotreport.com
www.showstudio.com
www.we-make-money-not-art.com
www.wired.com
www.yatzer.com

Magazines

Cabinet, Vogue, Art Review, ID, Domus, Frieze

Movies directors

David Cronenberg, Quentin Tarantino, Stanley Kubrick, Jim Jarmusch, David Keith Lynch

Designers, artists, technologists

Eve Hesse, Eva Ziesal, Alexander Girard, Donald Judd, Agnes Martin, Marcel Duchamp, Alexander Calder, Ted Muehling, Issey Miyake, NUNO, Makoto Koizumi, Despina Papadopoulos, Enki Bilal, Hussein Chalayan, Santiago Calatrava, Philip Beesley, Theo Jansen, Nikola Tesla, Frida Kahlo, Antony Gormley, Hans Bellmer, Ira Sherman

Books

Aldersey-Williams, Hugh & Hall, Peter & Sargent, Ted & Antonelli, Paola: Design and the Elastic Mind

Armstrong, John: The Secret Power of Beauty

Arnold, Janet: Patterns of Fashion 1: 1660-1860

Capra, Fritjof: The Hidden Connections: A Science for Sustainable Living

Csikszentmihalyi, Mihaly & Rochberg-Halton, Eugene:
            The Meaning of Things, Domestic Symbols and the Self

Didi-Huberman, Georges: Schädel sein

Dissanayake, Ellen: Homo Aestheticus: Where Art Comes From and Why

Dunne, Anthony: Hertzian Tales: Electronic Products, Aesthetic Experience, and Critical Design

Entwistle, Joanna: The Fashioned Body

Evans, Caroline & Menkes, Suzy & Polhemus, Ted & Quinn, Bradley: Hussein Chalayan

Frankel, Susannah: Visionaries, Interviews with Fashion Designers

Gallo , Donald R.: Owning It: Stories About Teens with Disabilities

Hallam, Elizabeth & Ingold, Tom: Creativity and Cultural Improvisation

Hara, Kenya: Designing Design

Haraway, Donna: Simians, Cyborgs, and Women: The Reinvention of Nature

Hodge, Brooke: Skin + Bones: Parallel Practices in Fashion and Architecture

Igoe, Tom & O'Sullivan, Dan: Physical Computing:
            Sensing and Controlling the Physical World with Computers

Jodidio, Philip: Santiago Calatrava: 1951: Architect, Engineer, Artist

Kac, Eduardo: Signs of Life. Bio Art and Beyond

Kuhn, Thomas S.: The Structure of Scientific Revolutions

Lee, Suzanne: Fashioning the Future

McDonough, William & Braungart, Michael: Cradle to Cradle: Remaking the Way We Make Things

McLuhan, Marshall: Understanding Media: The Extensions of Man

Newark, Tim: Camouflage

Papanek, Victor: Design for the Real World

Quinn, Bardley: The Fashion of Architecture

Reichle, Ingeborg: Kunst aus dem Labor

Semff, Michael & Spira, Anthony: Hans Bellmer

Shelley, Mary: Frankenstein

Sontag, Susan: On Photography

Steffen, Alex: Worldchanging: A User's Guide for the 21st Century

Tucker, Andrew: The London Fashion Book

Walker, Barbara G.: Sampler Knitting

Workman, Jane E. & Freeburg, Beth W.: Dress and Society

Bibliography

The comprehensive bibliography in my previous book is extended here.

Aldersey-Williams, Hugh & Hall, Peter & Sargent, Ted & Antonelli, Paola: Design and the Elastic Mind. The Museum of Modern Art New York, 2008.

Banzi, Massimo: Getting Started with Arduino. Make, 2008.

Barthes, Roland: The Language of Fashion. Berg Publishers, 2006.

Benyus, Janine: Biomimicry: Innovations Inspired by Nature. Harper Perennial, 2002.

Berzowska, Joanna: Electronic Textiles: Wearable Computers, Reactive Fashion, and Soft Computation. In Textile. The Journal of Cloth & Culture, Digital Dialogues 2, Vol. 3, No. 1, Jeffries, Janis (Ed.). Berg Publishers, 2005.

Beylerian, George M. & Caniato, Michele & Dent Andrew & Quinn, Bradley: Ultra Materials: How Materials Innovation Is Changing the World. Thames & Hudson, 2007.

Bolton, Andrew: Wild: Fashion Untamed. Metropolitan Museum of Art, 2004.

Bourriaud, Nicolas: Relational Aesthetics. Les Presse Du Reel, 1998.

Brownell, Blaine: Transmaterial 3: A Catalog of Materials that Redefine our Physical Environment. Princeton Architectural Press, 2010.

Busch, Otto von: FASHION-able: Hacktivism and Engaged Fashion Design. 2008.

Cho, Gilsoo: Smart Clothing: Technology and Applications (Human Factors and Ergonomics). CRC Press, 2009.

Cianfanelli, Elisabetta & Kuenen, Stoffel: Metamorphosis. Polistampa, 2010.

Clark, Andy: Natural-Born Cyborgs: Minds, Technologies, and the Future of Human Intelligence. Oxford University Press, 2003.

Clark, Judith & Teunissen, Jose & Nefkens, Han: The Art of Fashion: Installing Allusions. Museum Boijmans Van Beuningen, Rotterdam, 2009.

Csikszentmihalyi, Mihaly: Creativity: Flow and the Psychology of Discovery and Invention. Harper Perennial, 1997.

Fletcher, Kate: Sustainable Fashion and Textiles: Design Journeys. Earthscan Publications Ltd, 2008.

FoAM: .x-med-a, electronic edition, FoAM (Ed.). Roels NV, Belgium, 2006.

Fortunati, Leopoldina & Katz, James E. & Riccini, Raimonda: Mediating the Human Body: Technology, Communication, and Fashion. Routledge, 2003.

Hippel, Eric von: Democratizing Innovation. MIT Press, Cambridge, 2005.

Gray, Chris H.: Cyborg Citizen: Politics in the Posthuman Age. Routledge, 2002.

Gray, Chris H.: The Cyborg Handbook, Routledge, 1995.

Hauser, Jens: SK-INTERFACES: Exploding Borders in Art, Science and Technology (Story of the Mersery Poets). Liverpool University Press, 2008.

Igoe, Tom: Making Things Talk: Practical Methods for Connecting Physical Objects. Make, 2007.

Iwamoto, Lisa: Digital Fabrications: Architectural and Material Techniques (Architecture Briefs). Princeton Architectural Press, 2009.

Katz, James: Machines That Become Us: The Social Context of Personal Communication Technology. Transaction Publishers, 2006.

Kawamura, Yuniyara: Fashion-ology: An Introduction to Fashion Studies. Berg Publishers, 2005.

Klooster, Thorsten: Smart Surfaces – and Their Applications in Architecture and Design, Birkhäuser Architecture, 2009.

Kozel, Suzanne: Closer: Performance, Technologies, Phenomenology. The MIT Press, 2008.

Krumm, John: Ubiquitous Computing Fundamentals. Chapman & Hall, 2009.

Lawo, Michael & Pasher, Edna & Pezzlo, Rachel: Intelligent Clothing: Empowering the Mobile Worker by Wearable Computing. IOS Press, 2009.

Lewis, Alison: Switch Craft: Battery-Powered Crafts to Make and Sew. Potter Craft, 2008.

Maeda, John: Creative Code: Aesthetics + Computation. Thames & Hudson, 2004.

Maison Martin Margiela & Gaultier, Jean-Paul & Frankel, Susannah & Putman, Andrée, Beecroft, Vanessa: Maison Martin Margiela. Rizzoli, 2009.

Mattila, H. R.: Intelligent Textiles and Clothing. CRC Press, 2006.

Mau, Bruce: Life Style. Phaidon Press 2005.

Merleau-Ponty, Maurice: Phenomenology of Perception. Routledge, 2nd Edn., 2002.

Miah, Andy: Human Futures: Art in an Age of Uncertainty. Liverpool University Press, 2009.

Norman, Donald: Emotional Design: Why We Love (or Hate) Everyday Things. Basic Books, 2005.

Pakhchyan, Syuzi: Fashioning Technology: A DIY Intro to Smart Crafting. O'Reilly Media, 2008.

Pavitt, Jane: Fear and Fashion in the Cold War. Victoria & Albert Museum, 2008.

Pons, Jose L.: Wearable Robots: Biomechatronic Exoskeletons. Wiley, 2008.

Poslad, Stefan: Ubiquitous Computing: Smart Devices, Environments and Interactions. Wiley, 2009.

Quinn, Bradley: Textile Futures: Fashion, Design and Technology. Berg Publishers, 2010.

Reas, Casey & Fry, Ben: Processing: A Programming Handbook for Visual Designers and Artists. MIT Press, 2007.

Reichle, Ingeborg: Art in the Age of Technoscience, Genetic Engineering, Robotics, and Artificial Life in Contemporary Art. SpringerWienNewYork, 2009.

Rheingold, Howard: Smart Mobs: The Next Social Revolution, Basic Books, 2003.

Rucker, Rudy V. B.: Wetware. Eos, 1997.

Sakar, Tapan K. & Wicks, Michael C. & Salazar-Palma, Magdalena & Bonneau, Robert J.: Smart Antennas. Wiley-IEEE Press, 2003.

Seymour, Sabine: Fashionable Wearables. Aesthetic Interaction Interfaces. In Fashion in Context, Buxbaum, G. (Ed.), pp. 144 - 146. SpringerWienNewYork, 2009.

Seymour, Sabine: Fashionable Technology – The Intersection of Design, Fashion, Science, and Technology. SpringerWienNewYork, 2008a.

Seymour, Sabine: Fashionable Wearables – Design & Technology. In 360 Artifical Atlas of Austrian Design. Edited by designforumMQ, pp. 160 - 168. designforumMQ Wien, 2008b.

Seymour, Sabine: The Garment as Interface. In Handbook of Research on
User Interface Design and Evaluation for Mobile Technology, Vol. 1, Lumsden, J. (Ed.). pp. 176 - 186.
IGI
Global, 2008c.

Seymour, Sabine & Beloff, Laura: Fashionable Technology – The Next Generation of Wearables.
In The Art and Science of Interface and Interaction Design. Sommerer, Christa & Jain, Lakhmi C.
(Eds.), pp. 131 - 140. Springer, 2008.

Seymour, Seymour & Satomi, Mika: Designing our Extended Body. In Interface Cultures. Artistic
Aspects of Interaction, pp. 113 - 120. Transcript Verlag, 2008.

Steele, Valerie: Gothic: Dark Glamour. Yale University Press, 2008.

Teunissen, José & Brand, Jan: Fashion and Imagination, About Clothes and Art. ArtEZ Press, 2009.

Theng, Yin-Leng & Duh, Henry: Ubiquitous Computing: Design, Implementation and Usability
(Premier Reference Source). IGI Global, 2008.

Varshney, Upkar: Pervasive Healthcare Computing: EMR/EHR, Wireless and Health Monitoring.
Springer, 2009.

Vinken, Barbara: Fashion Zeitgeist – Trends and Cycles in the Fashion System. Berg Publishers,
2005.

Wallace, Gordon G. & Teasdale, Peter R. & Spinks, Geoffrey, M. & Kane-Maquire, Leon, A. P.:
Conductive Electroactive Polymers: Intelligent Materials Systems. CRC Press, 2002.

Warwick, Alexandra & Cavallaro, Dani: Fashioning the Frame. Boundries, Dress, and the Body. Berg
Publishers, 2001.

Wosk, Julie: Women and the Machine: Representations from the Spinning Wheel to the Electronic
Age. The John Hopkins University Press, 2003.

Wosk, Julie: Alluring Androids, Robot Women, and Electronic Eves. Fort Schuyler Press, 2008.

Xu, Yangsheng & Li, Wen Jung & Lee, Ka Keung: Intelligent Wearable Interfaces. Wiley, 2008.

Zylinska, Joanna: The Cyborg Experiments: The Extensions of the Body in the Media Age. Continuum
International Publishing Group, 2002.

Photo Credits

Numbers refer to pages on which illustrations appear

8 - 9: Thomas Voorn

Body Sculpture
22 - 25: Chris Moore, 26 - 27: Jacob Lillis, 28: Fabrice Lachant, 29: Jacob Lillis, 30 - 33: Jacob Barcala, 34, 36 - 37: Davide Farabegoli, 38 - 41: Rebecca Parks, 43: Alessandro Imbrogno, 44, 46 - 47: Philips, 48: Richard Burbridge, 50 - 51: Gavin Alexander, 52: Sas-Yve Trommler

The Garment as Amplifier of Fantasy
57: Chris Moore, 59: Ricardo O'Nascimento, 61 - 63: Özgür Albayrak, 65: Fee Arnold, 66 - 67: Bart Hess, 68: Peter Gaan, 70 - 71: Salazar Quas, 73: Soomi Park, 74 - 75: Julien Oppenheimer, 76 - 77: Marina Faust, 78 - 79: Ronald Stoops, 80: Dan Lecca, 81: Ronald Stoops

Scientific Couture
84 - 87: Matt Johnson, 89: Gary Cass, 91: Maarten Willemstein, 92 - 93: Lucy McRae, 94 - 95: Susanne Philippson, 96 - 98: Gary Wallis, 100 - 103: Sonja Bäumel, 104 - 105: Alexander Reeder

The Epidermis as Metaphor
108 - 109: Cait & Casey Reas, 110 - 111: Eelco Borremans, 113: J.B. Spector & Cute Circuit, 114 - 115: Pop Design, 116, 118 - 119: Kerri Wallace, 120: Zane Berzina, 122 - 123: David Rankalawon, 124 - 125: Mark Glassner, 127: ESKI

Acknowledgments

An attempt to list each person individually would certainly fail due to the sheer amount of wonderful individuals who motivated me to compile this book. Thus, a special thanks to everyone who has ever worked with me (or Moondial) in any capacity:

introduced me to projects, invited me to conferences, suggested we test a new product, acquainted me with a new technology, critically discussed with me the state of the art, let us try out a new material, sent me their new prototypes, requested that I evaluate a paper, developed research projects with us, solicited me to become a review board member, commented on my writings, hired us to consult, asked me to design new syllabi, afforded me to create a new research area – and to my former students all over the world that continue to work in this area and keep me posted on their developments.

Thanks to all the contributors for their submissions and valuable comments. And to all those who made the research for this book possible, in particular:

PARSONS THE NEW SCHOOL FOR DESIGN

Parsons The New School for Design
Fashionable Technology Lab
ft.parsons.edu

 interfaceculture

Kunstuniversität Linz
Interface Culture

Biography

Dr. Sabine Seymour is an innovator and trend spotter who focuses on next generation 'wearables' and the intersection between aesthetics and function. She is the chief creative officer of her company Moondial, which develops fashionable wearables and consults on fashionable technology to companies worldwide.

Sabine is the director of the Fashionable Technology Lab at Parsons The New School for Design in New York and educates at numerous institutions worldwide, including the University of Arts and Industrial Design in Linz, Austria.

Sabine serves as a jury and editorial review board member for many renowned institutions, conferences, and publications. She is widely published and curates, exhibits, and lectures internationally. She has received numerous grants and awards.

Index